I0421157

Vine of the Soul

By Dave Rebeck

Chapter 1

The Tea

No one emerges from an ayahuasca trance completely unchanged. Apprehension was high in the muted tones of Craig Hunt's dimly lit kitchen, where three men gathered around a small wooden table. The rust colored liquid in the clear glass jar on the table looked like dirty coffee, lightened slightly by cream. John Masters carefully unscrewed the lid and smelled the contents. He was greeted by an acrid, uniquely bitter aroma. His companions, Craig Hunt and Bob Timmons, gazed silently at the proceedings. Their apprehension was only slightly lifted by the smile that crept onto John's face.

Although both had experienced the LSD craze of the Seventies, the *tea* represented the ultimate excursion from reality, as the belief goes. The Vine of the Soul. The vehicle of travel, literally, between worlds. John had discovered it years ago while living in Brazil and he had succeeded in convincing Craig and Bob to experience it themselves. Initially, they had agreed enthusiastically. But now, in the moment of truth, they weren't so sure.

Ayahuasca, or yage, is not the typical recreational drug. While LSD was easily assimilated to the beer guzzling, Rock 'n Roll campus crowd, ayahuasca was shrouded in the veil of mystery associated with the shamans of the Amazon rain forest. When John advised Craig to lock the doors, turn on the answering machine, dim the lights and use the rest room one last time his anxiety deepened.

"You mean I won't be able to go to the bathroom if I need to?"

"You might. Then again, you might not be able to move at all. It depends on the person." John smiled.

"You mean we just lay here in a trance?" Bob was curious.

"Your body just lies here," replied John. "Your soul, however..." His arm swept out in a gesture that implied soaring away.

"What if someone comes to the door?" Craig was clinging to reality.

"Don't answer it. Interacting with the rest of the world is not a good idea for the next six to eight hours."

Craig and Bob exchanged glances. Suddenly this was becoming too strange. They were becoming overwhelmed with apprehension.

John took notice of this apparent change of heart and tried to reassure them. "Look, I've done this dozens of times. Trust me." He understood their anxiety and wanted to calm them without being pushy.

Certainly there was never any reason to doubt John's integrity. Trust was not a problem. Fear of the unknown was more like it. From a scientific standpoint, ayahuasca remains as mysterious as any drug known. It wasn't until 1851 that English Botanist Richard Spruce observed its use by Tukonoan tribes in the Rio Vaupes of Brazil. Use of the tea was the focal point of religious and shamanistic rites of tribal peoples in the northwestern region of the

Amazon basin from antiquity, traditions which are actively in place today.

Comprised of various combinations of hallucinogenic plants, ayahuasca's main ingredient, Banisteriopsis Caapi, is a thick liana, or vine, indigenous to the Amazon basin. Although fairly abundant in its natural setting it is not always easy to find or procure, and it is therefore cultivated. Among its active principles, not all of which have been identified, is the mysterious harmine, or telepathine, named for its purported telepathy imparting capabilities. In addition to Banisteriopsis, the tea is augmented with B. Rusbyana or Psychotria Viridis, among others. There are apparently dozens of variations of ayahuasca, differing in the type and intensity of the visions they produce.

Craig and Bob were not well versed on the medicinal chemistry of ayahuasca. In fact, John had still not explained how this concoction had found its way from the Amazon jungle to a suburban Ohio kitchen. For all they knew, this was just another of John's elaborate practical jokes. That is, until John began chanting in a language they had never heard before. As he poured the liquid into three small glasses, a portal to a new world was opening, ready to

embrace the three travelers.

Chapter 2

Northwest Amazon

The shaman sliced through the dense jungle foliage with the ease of a jaguar. His journey began with the sun's orange disk ascending over the eastern horizon more than two hours earlier. He was midway towards his destination when he stopped dead in his tracks. A few yards ahead in a small clearing lay the remains of a large animal. Stepping forward to investigate, he realized that the carcass was human, its skull still covered with skin and hair, matted with dried blood. He recognized the horrified visage, mouth open in a final, mute scream. His apprentice had disappeared the day before, his fate now eerily revealed. It was now the shaman's duty to complete his apprentice's ill fated mission: the procurement of the Banisteriopsis Caapi and Psychotria Viridis plants, the sacred ingredients used in ayahuasca, the mysterious medicinal tea of the Tuapano tribe.

Finally, after an otherwise uneventful journey, the ageless shaman reached his destination. Deep in the rain forest, darkened by the overhead canopy of vegetation, which blocked the relentless tropical sun, the shaman reached out to a liana. The thick woody vine snaked its way up to the canopy, hundreds of feet over the floor of the forest. Later explorers to the rain forest are amazed at the

darkness, even at midday, of the interior of the forest. Without rest

and on constant vigil for his apprentice's murderer, the medicine

man commences his task.

With crude tools fashioned from bone and tree limbs, the

shaman begins by furiously beating the base of the vine, all the while

chanting his respects to the soul of the vine. Little by little, the bark

of the Banisteriopsis vine begins to loosen and the shaman collects

the loosened shards in a ceremonial satchel. Although the technique

used to obtain the bark seems routine, collection of Banisteriopsis is

relegated to shamans or their apprentices. The power of the vine is

not taken lightly by the people in the region. Used in the proper

context, ayahuasca can heal or transport one's soul to realms outside

of normal consciousness, conferring health and providing solutions

to mortal conflicts. Used improperly, ayahuasca can kill. Quickly.

Several hours later, the shaman completes the collection

process. Bundling his prize material, he bows to pray to the vine of

the soul. Satisfied that his safe passage has been ensured, the

shaman begins to retrace his steps back to the village. He is hoping to reach his destination by nightfall. However, should darkness envelop the rain forest, the shaman knows that his night vision will guide him safely. Lifelong use of ayahuasca has increased his nighttime visual acuity to equal that of the big cats. Although not impenetrable, the shaman is revered as a fierce warrior. He will pass through the jungle unchallenged and unharmed.

Just minutes before the sun sets and nocturnal predators begin their hunt the shaman reaches the village. Set along a winding riverbank in a small clearing, the village consists of a dozen or so small grass huts with a large communal hut a few hundred yards in the distance. Without speaking or acknowledging the presence of others, the shaman strides deliberately toward his hut. Located at the edge of the forest, isolated from the main grouping, his hut is off limits except for the sick and dying. It is there that he sets down his load and, without food or rest, embarks on the sacred rite of ayahuasca preparation.

Back of his hut arranged in a single row, three large clay vats, each a meter across, lay waiting. Each sits atop a wood fire, suspended by thick branches arranged in an elaborate geometrical design. Each vat is filled with water and to each the shaman adds

the Banisteriopsis vine along with Psychotria Viridis and other

hallucinogenic plants. Through the night, in a solitary ritual, the

shaman repeats the process of boiling down the vines and isolating

the greenish liquid. By dawn, the shaman is exhausted. As the fires

smolder, he carefully grasps a large gourd that he has filled with

ayahuasca. He will sleep all day next to the ceremonial gourd and as

nightfall blankets the jungle once again, the shaman, with several

male members of the tribe, will drink the brew and take a journey

which transcends time and space.

That night with several fires burning around a small clearing, the

tribesmen gather around the gourd. The women and children are

kept at a safe distance in their huts. Soon chanting is heard as the

smoky campfires envelop the village.

"MO-MA-MO-MA" is repeated as the gourd is passed and each

tribesman drinks his share of the bitter tea.

Within minutes, a vague nauseous sensation gives way to mild

intoxication. As the night chorus of jungle beasts escalates to an

apparent crescendo, the ayahuasca grips the men. Hours on end, as the moon arcs over them, the tribesmen experience the visions.

Time his dissolved. For each, the journey is transformative and

healing. This is their religion, their connection to the grand power of

the universe. The shaman has guided them to the very real world of

spirits and above all, knowledge. They will be better men for it. As

the sun shocks the jungle with its brilliance, the men collapse in

exhaustion.

Chapter 3

Kelly

Five doors down from Craig Hunt's house, in a post modern style home situated cozily in a pine grove at the end of a winding driveway, a baby was crying. Not a "Mommy I'm hungry" or "Mommy my diaper needs changed" kind of cry. No, this was almost a malignant cry, the result of a pain that all parents wished they could experience in the place of their infants. Jason Ferguson was one day shy of four months old and had cried like this seemingly since the delivery. Kelly Ferguson, a first time mom, never felt so much distress, both for her baby and herself. Twenty-six and petite with full brown hair and liquid brown eyes to match, she was pretty enough for a magazine cover, or so thought her husband Kyle. Kyle Ferguson MD. Having just finished his residency and launching a private practice in internal medicine, his income would make it possible for Kelly to stay home and play mom. It was not exactly turning out to be the paradise she had anticipated. There are scant few activities worse that helplessly enduring the early months of a colicky baby. She felt sorry not for herself but for Jason. And with Kyle gone for fifty or sixty hours a week between his office and the hospital there was little reprieve.

Kelly had met Kyle at St. Luke's Hospital in nearby Logan. He was a resident, she was his patient. They hit it off from the start and dated soon after her release. The vague abdominal pain she was experiencing had disappeared before a diagnosis could be made. Kyle remembers clumsily examining a woman so attractive that his mind wandered. Kelly remembers a confident young doctor with graceful hands. They married two years to the date of her release.

Soon her pain would reemerge. But this time, a diagnosis and a bizarre treatment would conquer it once and for all. She would be ushered into a new world, at once horrifying and wonderful. And she would create a schism between herself and her hard working husband. She was not yet aware of this, but the Vine of the Soul was reaching out for her and her baby. In a matter of months the secrets of the ancient Amazon would reveal themselves to a frightened young mother and her suffering infant.

Chapter 4

Take Off

John picked up a glass of the tea and handed it carefully to Bob, then another to Craig. He picked up his own and looked at it as if examining a work of art. He looked at Bob and Craig and smiled broadly.

"Bottoms up, my friends." He raised his glass in a gesture beckoning the others to toast. They clanked their glasses and Craig and Bob watched John drink the entire glassful. They looked at each other for support, shrugged, and drank the nasty liquid. Both shuddered involuntarily from the aftertaste. It was perhaps the most disgusting substance that either had ever tasted. John filled his glass with tap water and poured a little into each of their glasses. He gestured for them to copy as he swirled the water to suspend the remaining residue and drank it down. With an effortless motion he took and washed all three glasses.

"Shall we?" He motioned for them to enter the family room.

"Is there something we can eat to get this nasty taste out of our mouths?" asked Craig.

"Unfortunately nothing works. Besides, the taste helps as a reality check during the trip."

Craig shook his head to indicate confusion.

"At any point during the visions, you may decide you want to come back for a while. That's okay. To do that just open your eyes. The after taste of the tea will remind you that this is a drug-induced phenomenon. Then close your eyes again and away you go." John was so matter of fact he could have been explaining the workings of a lawn tractor rather than describing the effects of a hallucinogenic drug. It did little to relax his friends.

"Don't forget, this only lasts four to six hours. You'll probably wish it didn't end so quickly."

Bob wasn't convinced. *But there's no turning back now.*

"Let's get comfortable," said John. "Sitting or lying down is the best method."

The three men selected their respective chairs and settled in. It had been fifteen minutes since they drank the tea. The summer sun was setting behind a bank of maple trees next to Craig's house.

"How long?" Craig was suddenly anxious for the experience to begin.

"One-half to one hour. You'll know." John smiled.

Craig Hunt leaned back in his recliner in anticipation. He could imagine molecules of harmine finding his bloodstream and coursing their way to his brain. If ayahuasca really changed brain chemistry, as he had heard, then what type of changes would occur? He refused to believe that John would expose his friends to anything dangerous.

Craig had known John since high school. Despite his strong academic record, John decided to go into the navy out of high school. He firmly believed in seeing the world before settling down. Deep down, he doubted he ever would just settle down. During many of his weekends off he would hook up with Craig to enjoy the campus atmosphere at Michigan State, where Craig was studying law. It was there that he met Craig's friend, Bob Timmons. The three had become quite close toward the end of their respective military and collegiate careers, heading off on numerous camping adventures. Craig felt that there was no more trustworthy person in his life than John. There was nothing to worry about. Period.

Suddenly, it was like a light switch being turned on, or more accurately, a viewing screen to a new dimension being activated. Craig could see John smiling at him from across the room. All at once he perceived John as his closest ally and a completely alien life form. His ambivalence was about to dissolve in the infinity of existence. His friend was a shaman, guiding him to a higher world.

Chapter 5

The Good Doctor

Kyle Ferguson arrived at the hospital promptly at 7:30 AM.

St. Luke's Hospital was located twelve miles from their home, but it

was almost all expressway so even in heavy traffic he only had a

twenty minute commute. He still drove his 1984 Ford Escort that

had faithfully transported him throughout his residency. He shook his head as he entered the physician's parking area--his beater hardly

belonged next to the Mercedes' and BMW's. He had decided that

Kelly and Jason needed a new van much more than he needed an

import. His Escort would have to do for at least three more years.

Grabbing his briefcase from the passenger seat he realized that

he had forgotten his lunch at home. Cafeteria food again. He vowed

that once he had completed his residency he would swear off

cafeteria food. Famous last words. Nearing the nurse's station he

was glad to see his favorite ward clerk, Nancy Mullins. She knew

that Kyle was not a morning person and she kept the conversation to

a minimum until noon or so.

"Good morning, Doctor," she said cheerfully.

"Morning, sunshine." Kyle was in a better mood than usual.

"Coffee's fresh." Nancy motioned to the back room. A mother

of four herself, Nancy knew firsthand what Kyle and Kelly were

going through with Jason. Sleepless nights are a part of the

parenthood package, and for health professionals it's imperative that they leave their private lives at home. Sleep or no sleep, the patients must come first.

Kyle was also confident that his residency was a proving ground for his ability to work under stressful conditions with little sleep. Despite the growing criticism levied at the medical profession for imposing rigorous work schedules for residents, Kyle privately felt great satisfaction at having survived the ordeal. Twenty-four hour work shifts had certainly conditioned his mind and body for the rigorous lifestyle of physician and new father.

Nancy had already stacked three patient charts on the shelf at the nurse's station. Her efficiency was unequaled. Kyle knew it when she was off duty and the other ward clerks tried to fill her shoes. If it wasn't for the vacation and benefits she enjoyed at the hospital he'd try to coax her to work for him in private practice.

"Mrs. Dunning is scheduled for an ECG at eleven. You should probably examine her first." Nancy smiled as she handed Kyle Mrs. Dunning's chart.

Kyle began reading the chart as he headed for Mrs. Dunning's room--504. White female, age seventy-eight, five foot four, one hundred eighty pounds. History of cardiac problems. Admitted July 16, two days ago. Complained of difficulty breathing. Maintenance medication consisting of Lasix 40mg daily, Lanoxin 0.25mg daily, and a potassium supplement. Diagnosis: Congestive Heart Failure.

Despite the ominous sounding name, CHF is not necessarily a death knell. The heart is in the process of failing, not in sudden failure. Put simply, the cardiac muscle is no longer able to adequately pump blood throughout the circulatory system. Eventually, blood begins to pool as the tired heart fails to push the blood through the extremities hard enough. The patient experiences swollen ankles and difficulty breathing as the lungs labor against the additional fluid. In time, the heart does fail completely, but with medication that can be postponed indefinitely, at least several years. Lasix, a diuretic, causes the kidneys to increase volume and frequency of urination, ridding the body of excess fluid. Along with urine, the patient loses potassium, which then needs to be supplemented. Commonly, the drug digoxin is used to strengthen the force of the heartbeat and slow down the heart rate. Kyle

remembered digoxin from his pharmacology books as being derived

from the foxglove plant--old time medicine meets modern

technology.

Kyle entered the room to find Mrs. Dunning just finishing her

salt restricted breakfast. She looked up at him with suspicion. Many

patients never get used to the parade of doctors typical of teaching

hospitals.

"Good morning Mrs. Dunning, I'm Dr. Kyle Ferguson."

"Pleasure." She was a bit sarcastic.

"Has your breathing improved any?" he asked. Her ankles were

exposed and almost grotesquely swollen. Her condition did not

appear to be improving.

"Not a bit. This breakfast was terrible." She sighed. To a

lifelong table salt abuser, a bland sodium free diet is practically

tasteless.

"Hopefully, we'll get you back on your feet and into your own

kitchen soon." Kyle was being optimistic. He pulled his

stethoscope from around his neck and listened to her labored breathing.

"We may have to increase your Lasix, Mrs. Dunning."

"Oh no, Not again." She shook her head.

"We'll see if we can get rid of that extra fluid. I'm sure you'd feel much better." Kyle patted her swollen ankles. "You'll have to learn to like bland food as well. Salt is not your friend I'm afraid."

"You're the boss." She smiled. *At least this guy has a little personality.*

Kyle began writing in her chart. He felt she needed Lasix intravenously, or IV Push, for extra effect, but figured the cardiologist should make that final decision later in the day. He made his recommendations based on his superficial examination and headed for the nurse's station.

"Next." He filled his cup almost automatically.

"512. Peptic ulcer." Nancy handed him the next chart.

Kyle was a little excited about this patient. Tom Monahan was thirty-five years old and was admitted with a recurrent ulcer. After years of expensive symptomatic therapy, his ulcers remained

basically incurable. Originally thought to occur due to excess

stomach acid, physicians could not understand why most people

could tolerate incredibly strong stomach acid while ulcer patients

would succumb to the destruction of their stomach lining. Clearly,

there was more to the picture than acid. The breakthrough came

about five years ago when researchers in Australia discovered that

the bacterium Helicobactor Pylori could be isolated from ninety

percent of ulcer patients. From that discovery came the possible

cure. Known as Triple Therapy, the trio of the drugs metronidazole,

tetracycline, and bismuth subsalicylate given for two weeks would

wipe out H. Pylori infection and theoretically would rid the ulcer

patients of the disease completely. Kyle had registered to test the

new protocol with some of his patients. So far the results were

encouraging. Monahan was the first ulcer patient that Kyle had tried

the therapy on. He entered 512.

"And how's that gut of yours?" Kyle was sure the reply would

be positive.

"I don't know," said Monahan. "I don't feel pain but I still feel like crap."

" Could be the antibiotics. In one more week we'll do a scope. I bet you'll be pleasantly surprised."

"Thanks Doc. I'd like to get outta here before Christmas." Monahan managed a smile.

Kyle nodded and signed off his chart. Cures were becoming few and far between. He relished the ones he observed. If the experimental protocol worked it could become common practice. After making his rounds, he decided to call Kelly. Maybe he could go out for lunch. As he dialed from the nurse's station he hoped he didn't catch her in a valuable napping phase. Strangely, there was no answer. Maybe dinner was a possibility. With that, he grabbed his briefcase and headed to the Professional Building East, the home to his new office. An afternoon of chart reading and consults awaited him. By eight o'clock he was more than ready to go home.

Chapter 6

Visions

The chronology of the first ayahuasca experience for Craig was fragmented at best. Although his first reaction upon emerging from the drug's effects were negative, in the days that followed he began to experience subtle yet definitive clues that something dramatic and positive had taken place that night. In contrast to the hedonistic highs that accompanied his previous drug experiences, the tea had not provided a pleasure trip at all, but rather, a glimpse into a world that was very real--a world of knowledge rather than pleasure.

He vividly recalls settling into his recliner and glimpsing at objects in the family room as he waited. Then, suddenly, he had the distinct feeling that he had transported to a completely new realm.

There weren't any hallucinations but visions--visions so vivid that Craig was completely convinced that he was experiencing co-existence in different worlds. On one hand, he would look at his friends across the room, and on the other hand, he would get glimpses of unfamiliar landscapes and people. Closing his eyes would send him soaring. He remembers directing himself, twenty feet or so off the ground, down the road and into a ravine at the end of his block. The terrain was very familiar, and the sensation of flight was unmistakably real. Then, inexplicably, he would find himself gazing upon a tall slender mountain peak punctuated with waterfalls and people: actually, women. Naked women. One of them appeared over and over. She was an attractive brunette whose face was familiar, but from where? And why was she crying?

Craig opened his eyes. He looked at his watch. What seemed like hours took fifteen minutes. He squeezed his hands into fists and opened them several times. He swiveled his ankles. It was him, alright. He felt that if he wanted to get out of the chair he could, but he had no desire to do so. One aspect of the experience that would persist for days was the essence of the tea itself. Craig noticed that what at first seemed like the odor of the ayahuasca on his breath was really the permeation of tea in the room and throughout his body--in effect, the atmosphere of the room had been replaced by the ayahuasca essence. He closed his eyes again.

For Bob Timmons, the ayahuasca didn't wear off soon enough. Having been out late the night before after a stressful week at work, he would have been better off watching a movie and dozing on his couch all night. An exhausting experience with a potent tropical hallucinogen was too much for him to handle. All night he struggled against the nausea and fleeting images that flashed before him. Closing his eyes, he eased himself out of his chair and onto the floor. That only seemed to precipitate further nausea and dysphoria. Images of his ex-wife beckoning to him didn't exactly improve the situation. Fighting the relentless vertigo, he resisted vomiting several times. Finally, as the visions eased up and the tea loosened its grip, Bob was overtired. He could only lie there, on the floor, wanting to be overtaken by sleep but badgered by the lingering traces of harmine in his bloodstream. Never again, never again.

John Masters smiled at his friends. Having experienced the positive impact of ayahuasca use, he understood the unpredictability that the drug exhibits in first time users. He knew from experience that even the worst side effects would be erased by the life enhancing properties of the tea. Bob had probably been caught on a bad night. But he would tell by watching Craig that something important was being transmitted to his friend. Craig's being was tapping into the vine.

Craig watched as Bob fidgeted on the floor. Is he OK? Turning to John, Craig watched in amusement as his friend sat perfectly still, eyes moving as if watching a movie from within his head. OK. Time for another flight. By now, Craig was accustomed to the routine. Eyes open for a reality check, eyes closed for a journey. Sometimes he was able to control individual "flights" and other times he relinquished control and went along for the ride, destination unknown. The singular notable vision was the recurrence of the brunette on the side of the unusual mountain peak, crying out to him. He knew the face from somewhere. He had to find out for sure.

By two o'clock, Bob and John were fast asleep. Craig was enjoying the last vestiges of intoxication. Having endured the ayahuasca experience without incident, he was determined to travel back to the mountain and communicate with the mystery girl. He wasn't having any luck. Opening his eyes, he looked at his watch. He'd been sitting practically motionless for almost six hours. Twisting in the recliner, his body was so stiff and sore it felt like he just went twelve rounds with George Foreman. Throughout the evening, John had been up and around, providing changes in the mood music on the tape player and bringing glasses of water for anyone who wanted them. On several occasions he would begin chanting in sounds that to Craig were unintelligible.

Finally, it was time to get up. Deciding to leave Bob and John where they were, Craig hoped a splash or two of cold water would erase the pasty look on his weary face. He was wrong. Deciding he didn't have the energy to brush his teeth, he negotiated his way to the master bedroom. Collapsing on his bed fully clothed, he felt as though he could sleep through an atomic blast. Fragmented images of the girl drifted in his mind's eye. Inexplicably Craig felt drawn to that image. Soon he would discover her identity. In the process,

their lives would become entangled and life would never be the

same. As the final vestige of the ayahuasca visions drifted away,

Craig succumbed to his exhaustion.

Chapter 7

Jason

In what is surely a part of the grand scheme of nature, it is virtually impossible to ignore a crying baby. After all, a crying baby is trying to communicate a want or a need that anyone in earshot should love to satisfy. However, if your baby happens to be colicky and cries almost twenty hours a day, you begin to feel like the grand scheme of nature is a crock of shit.

Kelly Ferguson was beginning to feel like she was the butt of a very bad joke. She loved her baby as much as any mother loved a child. That was all the more reason she felt his crying was nearing the unbearable stage. She'd heard the rhetoric over and over. That all babies cried a lot. That crying a lot doesn't injure the colicky baby, that there was no consensus as to the cause of colic let alone a cure. She'd heard that colicky babies develop into normal children. She'd even been told that the evidence suggested that a high percentage of intelligent children were colicky babies. And she felt like gouging out the eyes of the next person who guaranteed that she'd never remember Jason's colicky period. She was stressed-- completely.

Part of the problem, of course, was that Kyle was so busy. She knew that being the wife of a doctor would entail great loneliness. She could handle the alone time with no problem. It was the child rearing responsibilities that were taking their toll. Occasionally her mother would come by to give support, which was a big help. But Kelly couldn't help but feel that Kyle had no idea what she was going through. He had tried various remedies, such as simethicone, peppermint spirits, and even a prescription drug called Levsin. Nothing worked. Privately, Kyle was beginning to wonder if Jason actually did have an obstruction or other problem and not colic at all. Not to worry his young wife, he kept that thought to himself.

Jason's development seemed normal. Kelly nursed him on demand and his growth chart indicated that he was in the eighty-percentile; pretty healthy indeed. In fact, at twenty pounds, he looked a little chubby. His hair was coming in brown and very fine.

It was decided that he was an exact hybrid of his parents--sharing the features of both without looking terribly much like either.

Kelly was never much of an errand runner. Before Jason, she could busy herself at home with no problem. She had to quit her job at the library a few months before she got pregnant in order to decorate their new home. The envy of her friends, it was the fringe benefit of being a doctor's wife--his income would do just fine. She was excited about his completing his residency and had assumed his newly launched private practice would consume a lot of his time and energy. She wasn't prepared for the reality of it all, though.

Sometimes, the walls of their home would begin to close in on her, despite its enormity. At first, Kelly almost thought that they bit off more than they could chew. Situated in a rural area near Logan, sixty miles south of Columbus, it had five bedrooms, three bathrooms and a combination of rooms on the first floor that were as yet unassigned. It was the scenic beauty of the Appalachian foothills that caught their eye, and a two-acre backyard had playground written all over it. Kelly thought at times that it was too peaceful.

On this day, she decided to take Jason for a ride and run a few

errands. She had discovered in his third week that car rides were

soothing and they were definitely more interesting to Kelly than

sitting his car seat on the dryer and running that for a while. Ten

thirty. She would have them both dressed and out the door in half an

hour. Glancing out the kitchen window she noted the temperature on

the thermometer--eighty-two degrees. She picked up Jason and

brought him to her breast to nurse, which he obliged enthusiastically.

Five minutes later he fell sound asleep and she buckled him into his

car seat. Instantly, he began to scream. Ignoring him, Kelly picked

up the diaper bag, grabbed Jason and headed for their van.

Fortunately, by the time she reached the end of her street, Jason had

fallen back asleep. For now. Traveling east on Foote Road, she

headed for the post office. It was an unusually clear day, with wispy

clouds contrasting against a deep blue summer sky. Jason had been

sleeping soundly for half an hour and she took advantage of the

respite from his crying by taking the scenic route. She felt safe

leaving him in the van while she went inside the post office. Upon

returning to the van, she mischievously gave thought to taking a long

drive through the foothills, but decided to get home and play
housewife.

Just as she turned onto her street Jason woke up with his
incessant shrieking. It was time for his afternoon feeding. She noted
with absent-minded curiosity that the young lawyer down the block
had several cars in his driveway. It looked like the beginnings of a
weekend party. As she passed Craig's house, she instinctively
peered into his driveway and backyard. She shook her head. *Oh, to
be single again.*

Pulling into her driveway, she wondered how Kyle's day was
going. She knew it must be hard for him to go so long each day
without seeing Jason. She was proud of his work ethic and knew it
would pay off someday. Parking next to the front walk, Kelly got
out and rounded the van to Jason's side. Opening his door, she was
greeted by an experience that only a parent could enjoy. Jason
stopped crying momentarily, displayed an expression of joy in
recognizing his mom's face, held out his tiny, fragile arms to her and
with his eyes said "Mommy, I want you."

Chapter 8

The Day After

The morning sun held promise for a picturesque day. The instant Craig opened his eyes he felt completely awake. As he so often had to do he lay in bed for a second to determine what day it was and whether or not he had to go to work. Realizing he still had all of his clothes on from the previous day, the memories of a strange night bombarded him. That and the essence of ayahuasca still on his breath combined to verify his status: Ayahuasca experience, house guests downstairs, Saturday morning of a weekend off in July. He was a happy man.

Standing up he nearly kicked his cat Ritchie off the bed by accident. The startled cat purred instantly as Craig's fingers scratched between his ears. When asked what kind of cat he had, Craig liked to reply *instapurr*. At the slightest hint of human attention, Ritchie would purr loudly. Craig had never been a cat lover until the bedraggled stray showed up at his back deck one morning. A cup of milk later and they were best of friends. Craig turned to look in the mirror.

Although mostly sober since college, Craig still enjoyed the occasional bender. Unfortunately, he would usually suffer immensely for it the day after. This time, however, was markedly different. He felt sore, for sure, from sitting so long in one position. But his mind felt strangely lucid, accompanied by an increased visual acuity that delighted him. For some reason, he felt better than he could ever remember feeling. The stiffness wore off with a little activity, and putting on fresh clothes he felt as though he owned the world. He delayed his shower until his guests were up and about. He looked at his watch as he headed for the stairs: it was ten. John and Bob were sunning themselves on his deck like a couple of lizards. They had already made a pot of coffee and finished half of it.

"Well, look who decided to climb out of bed." Bob smiled and looked at his watch. "Hell, the day's half over."

Remembering what appeared to be a terrible experience for Bob, Craig was relieved to find him in a good mood.

"Hey man, have any good dreams?" John was also in an incredibly good mood. Craig then realized that he could not recall any dreams.

"No, I don't think so."

"You will." John started laughing.

"So what's on the agenda?" Craig was pounding his fist into his hand, ready to go.

"We thought you could give us a tour of your neighborhood. Good morning for a walk, if that's OK. Then maybe some chow, and then you name it." John gestured in an anything goes manner.

Craig had many questions about the tea, but figured that John would discuss it later. For now, he reveled in the camaraderie of his friends, the laziness of the weekend and the hot sun emanating from the crystal blue skies. He was still young enough to remember how to enjoy his weekends off.

"Let's go." He smiled at them.

Craig had found his house driving around one day. He wasn't really looking that seriously but when he saw "OPEN HOUSE" on the Realtor's sign he had nothing to lose. His street was L shaped, the outer edge bordering a ravine that abutted a state park. His house was near the corner of the L, with a back yard that overlooked a breathtaking ravine down to the stream below. He knew right away he wanted the house and was pleased to learn that the owners, whose elderly father had recently passed away, were anxious to sell. It was a quiet neighborhood and he loved the wooded privacy. For his city dwelling friends, Craig's house was a weekend getaway.

Although he had neighbors, they generally kept to themselves. In fact, in the three years he lived there, he had only briefly met some of his neighbors. They were all friendly in passing but felt no need to commune. Later, Craig would remark that the last thing he would have expected was to have been spied upon, yet his house was under scrutiny that very moment.

"Need anything?" Bob asked as they prepared for their stroll.

"Nope. All set," Craig replied.

"Want the doors locked?" John asked.

"No one's going to bother us." Craig waved him off. He was mistaken.

They walked as a group into the street, as there were no sidewalks. With the July sun heating up the day, Craig felt as if he could walk for hours. Then he noticed something very strange. At first he couldn't put his finger on it. There was something about the trees. As he looked at trees around him and especially in the distance, he had the unmistakable feeling that he was communicating with them, or perhaps that he was connected to them somehow.

John noticed Craig's fascination. "You noticed the trees." He was smiling broadly. "It's like they're talking to you isn't it?"

"Yeah, it's weird, but I like it," Craig said.

"It'll last for days, weeks, maybe forever," said John. "You'll never look at trees the same way."

"It's almost like they have personalities," Bob joined in.

"They do," said John. "The tea revealed it to you."

They kept walking. Despite the weirdness of it all, Craig felt good about the whole experience. Physically, there were no ill effects, and his mental clarity indicated that a positive change had taken place. He needed to study it more thoroughly.

"We can turn back here," Craig said. "It's getting to be about chow time." His friends agreed.

They crossed over to the other side of the road and retraced their path. The houses were all from different styles and most were far back from the street. They studied the varied architecture. Approaching the bend near Craig's house, they came near one of the newer homes on the block, built only ten years ago. The tall pines in the front yard were trimmed way up so that the house was visible beneath them. The men noticed a young mother working in her yard, with an automatic swing soothing her baby to sleep next to her. Craig stared momentarily and gasped, stopping abruptly.

"What is it?" asked John, startled.

Craig simply couldn't move, even though he wanted to in order to avoid attracting the young woman's attention. Instead, she gazed back and their eyes locked in a conspicuous, uncomfortable stare.

He had never seen her before, yet there, in the glistening noonday sun, was the girl in his ayahuasca visions. It was unmistakable.

John was a little embarrassed. "Come on dude, let's get some grub and have a talk."

"OK, OK." Craig finally broke his stare and headed forward towards his house. He felt a powerful sensation, as though he were suddenly energized.

"That's her, man. I saw her all night in my visions." Craig was noticeably agitated. "She needs us, I'm telling you, I think she needs us."

As they turned into Craig's driveway, the intruder quickly finished taking samples out of the jar on the kitchen table. He had what he felt would be enough for a spectroscopic exam and slipped unnoticed off the deck into the ravine as Craig and his cohorts returned. Two milliliters of ayahuasca were soon to be analyzed in a secure government laboratory and the mystery deepened.

Chapter 9

Hallucinogens

On Monday morning Craig awoke before his alarm.

Fortunately, his caseload was light this week, because for some

reason he felt terribly unmotivated. It bothered him that some days

he could simply not psyche himself up for work. He was afraid that

his mid-collegiate change in major was turning out to be a poor

decision. He had started with an enthusiastic bend toward

anthropology, a discipline which consumed three years of college.

At that point, it took little market research to conclude that anthropology was not the most lucrative career. The grim job prospects quickly dampened his enthusiasm for the studies of ancient man. Although it pained him to admit it, law was the way to go. With his high grade point average, acceptance into law school was not an obstacle, and his studies of the history of mankind gave way to the history of mankind's rules and laws.

He was prepared for the peon status of rookie attorney, but it seemed it would last forever. The prestige of law partnership would have to wait until he'd paid his dues as a rookie associate. But it was steady work with a steady paycheck, and he could write up divorce papers as well as anyone. In fact, he'd handled so many divorces that it steered him away from marriage himself. He was a young, single lawyer with a home almost in the country--could be worse.

Signing out with the firm's secretary, Craig left his closet sized office on the second floor of Branson, Branson, and McCullough, and decided to spend a rainy afternoon in the county library. His ayahuasca experience still fresh in his mind, Craig was hungry for information on the drug. He had revived his interest in anthropology, appreciating the fact that the study of mankind invariably involved the study of plant drugs. The two were intertwined inseparably since ancient times.

Pulling into the library's parking lot, Craig was pleased to find the lot almost empty. He chuckled to himself--having spent so many hours in the law library at college he was amused by his sudden realization that he had no idea where to begin once inside. It had been years, too many to remember, since he last stepped foot in a public library. He remembered something about a card file and the Dewey decimal system, then shook his head as he steered through the revolving doors.

He was shocked by what he saw. Constructed only five years ago, this was not what he remembered as a gradeschooler. Before him was a modern facility, replete with a dozen computer terminals and walls of software. On a far wall he noticed popular videos to borrow, and a side room was labeled "PC". There was not a card file anywhere, including the memory banks of the young lady in tight jeans who must be, perish the thought, a librarian.

He approached the counter. "Excuse me."

"Can I help you?" The young lady looked up and smiled.

"How long does it take to get a library card?" Craig asked.

"Two minutes. Do you have a driver's license?"

"Sure." Craig fished through his wallet. "There you go."

Two minutes later he was admiring his shiny new library card.
Bravely he approached one of the computer terminals.

HIT ANY BUTTON AND ENTER

He hit the letter "J". The screen promptly displayed a menu.

A) TITLE

B) AUTHOR

C) SUBJECT

Craig typed "C".

ENTER FIRST THREE OR MORE LETTERS OF SUBJECT

AYA (ENTER)

NOT FOUND

YAGE (ENTER)

NOT FOUND

Craig realized this might not be as easy as he'd hoped. He was embarrassed to ask for help in locating books on the subject of major hallucinogens, so he forged ahead.

HALLUCINOGEN (ENTER)

The screen went blank for a second, then began scrolling a series of titles about hallucinogens. There were fourteen titles, all with similar decimal numbers. He wrote several down and quickly erased the screen. Heading to the bay labeled 114:500 – 114:700 he began checking titles. Choosing several, he made his way for a table off in the corner and began his research.

Although most of the books were quite dated, the fact was that very little information had been recently published in mainstream titles, so the older books were still valuable. Several names popped up in different volumes, so he concentrated on the research by those men; Schultes, Spruce, Hofmann, Weil, Grinspoon, and McKenna, all luminaries in the field of drug research.

After several hours, Craig had amassed a great deal of information on most hallucinogens, with one notable exception: ayahuasca. Little was known about this curious tea, which piqued his interest further. He glanced at his notes as he sipped a cup of coffee.

There were various methods of classification, which were based on origin, chemical properties, routes of administration and even the types of hallucinations they induced. According to Weil, an effective breakdown was to separate them into two groups. The adrenaline-like compounds, which included phenylethylamines like mescaline in peyote and various synthetics, versus the indole containing compounds such as LSD and the tryptamines such as psylocibin in Magic Mushrooms. The fifth book in Craig's stack, Plants of Magic, was the only volume with any detailed information on ayahuasca.

Although he'd decided to borrow the book, he sat glued to his chair. Ayahuasca was certainly in a class by itself, although related to the tryptamines. Craig learned that there were several varieties of

Banisteriopsis vines used to prepare yage, as it is sometimes called,

and that there were equally numerous additive plants, all with

hallucinatory properties themselves added to Banisteriopsis to

complete the brew. The most common of these was a plant with the

interesting name Psychotria Viridis. Chemical analysis of yage

samples that Richard Spruce had sent back to England in the 1850's

form the Rio Vaupes revealed a drug in the beta carboline class,

which was called harmine. Psychotria Viridis was found to contain

N, N Dimethyltryptamine, or DMT.

The combination of harmine and DMT was apparently the key

to ayahuasca's properties. The amazing aspect of the tea is that

DMT is not active by mouth, as it is quickly destroyed by an enzyme

known as monoamine oxidase. However, harmine inhibits this

enzyme, allowing the DMT to reach the central nervous system.

From an anthropological standpoint, it is remarkable that the

primitive peoples of the Amazon rain forest were able to exploit

such a complex chemical reaction. Instantly, Craig remembered the

reasons he wanted to study anthropology in the first place.

He wanted to read on, but decided it was dinnertime, so he collected his belongings and headed for the desk. He'd been there so long there was a shift change at the check out counter.

"I'll take this one please," Craig said as he shoved the book along with his new card toward the skinny teenager at the opposite end of the counter. Craig waited for a reaction to the title of the book Plants of Magic but received none.

"Have a nice day. See you in two weeks."

"Thank you." Craig grabbed his book and headed out. He was already intrigued with what he'd found out. The combining of various plants to produce a tea of such a dramatic nature as ayahuasca was fascinating to him. He had to learn more. As he pulled out of the parking lot, his gaze was locked on the trees in the distance. They were talking to him.

Chapter 10

Kyle and Kelly

Kyle Ferguson pulled his Escort into the driveway and, easing past Kelly's van, parked in the back of the house. It was a warm summer evening. With the sun still shining past eight-thirty, there was still enough daylight to enjoy the great outdoors with his family. Although he'd brought several patient charts home with him, he instinctively knew that he'd probably not even open his briefcase. For now, all he could think about was Kelly, Jason, and a cold beer.

Entering the back door, he was greeted with the aroma of marinating chicken and charcoal. Kelly had prepared everything so it would be ready to go as soon as Kyle arrived--she never knew exactly when to expect him. He entered the kitchen and quietly snaked his arm around Kelly's waist, planting a kiss on her cheek.

"Sleeping?" he asked.

"Yeah, in his crib, too," she exclaimed. In addition to his fussiness, Jason rarely slept in his crib. Night after night, Kelly and Kyle had to get used to their infant between them in bed.

Although he looked forward to seeing his son, Kyle was just as happy to relax for awhile and share the time exclusively with Kelly.

"Want to give me a hand?" She was loaded with chicken.

Kyle opened the door onto the back patio, then disappeared into the kitchen. Returning to the patio, he triumphantly popped open a cold beer.

"Cooking purposes." He gestured to his Budweiser.

"Uh huh." She smiled with mock disgust. "You're supposed to use warm, flat beer."

"Well, this'll have to do. Why don't you join me?" Kyle asked.

She gestured to the mug on the picnic table. "Beat you to it."

"How was he today?" Kyle asked.

"The same. He slept a lot while I worked outside," she said. "I'm almost getting used to it."

"What did you try today?" he asked.

"Peppermint. Two doses." She sipped her beer.

Treatment of colic has become controversial in recent years. Most doctors agree that drug therapy should always be a last resort in infants. With colic, it's often difficult to convince parents of this. Therefore, most pediatricians like to try something therapeutic--if nothing else, it gives the parents a psychological boost, giving then the fleeting illusion that they are doing something. Kyle didn't mind the simethicone drips. Used in adults to break up gas bubbles, it works entirely in the gut, not getting absorbed into the bloodstream. In children, it is only somewhat effective. Levsin, an anticholinergic agent, slows motility in the gut and acts as a general antispasmodic in adults. In children it is available in a dropper bottle and used frequently, but with mixed results. Some doctors will even prescribe phenobarbital to calm the screaming baby, a practice that made Kyle cringe.

Peppermint spirits, on the other hand, were both safe and somewhat effective. For centuries, various species of the mint family had been known as folk remedies for upset stomach (after-dinner mint, anyone?) and Kyle had seen spirits of peppermint mentioned in a natural health publication he read from time to time.

Mixing a few drops in water and giving it to the infant it usually had an immediate effect. In Jason it induced a rather loud, adult sounding, minty belch which had to make him feel better. Most importantly, as a natural remedy, it had few, if any, side effects.

"Imagine, one day soon he'll wake up without colic," she said optimistically while turning the chicken. "I don't think we'll know how to behave."

With that, as if on cue, they were greeted by the screams of their now wide awake infant.

"You didn't think we'd be able to eat alone, did you?" She smiled as she walked past Kyle to get Jason. Kyle followed her with his eyes as she left the patio. His devotion grew the more he realized what she was going through every day. She returned with Jason in her arms.

"If you'll finish the chicken, I'll nurse him," she said, grabbing her beer. Kelly was not upset to have learned from various sources that drinking beer boosted milk production in nursing mothers. Kyle had doubted it from the start, but enjoyed sharing a beer or two with his wife. Just like the old days, he'd decided.

The two used to love going out, dining, dancing and drinking. Kyle had rarely dated in the early days of med school, and only slightly more once graduating. He had almost gotten used to the bachelor life when Kelly hit him like a Mack truck. Kyle remembers their first few dates like they were yesterday.

Finishing his beer, he held up his can. "Remember two-for-one night at the Outpost?" he asked.

"I'll never forget the boilermakers, that's for sure." She mocked throwing up. "You sure knew how to show a girl a good time."

"Need one more?" He gestured to her mug on his way past. She nodded. "Chicken's almost ready."

She looked down at Jason and smiled. Sometimes she felt like one big breast. If nothing else, nursing him through dinner meant having Kyle serve her. It was a fair trade off.

"You know, we should have a cookout and invite a few of our neighbors." She remembered seeing Craig a few days back.

"Yeah, we could do that. What made you think about doing that?" he asked curiously.

"I don't know. Just sounded fun."

As Kyle laid out the meal in front of Kelly, the sun began to disappear behind the trees. Immediately, the mosquitoes began their assault.

Kyle noticed Kelly swatting the pests. "Want to go in?" he asked.

"No, let's stick it out. It's so nice out here."

They finished eating in silence. Cleaning up the table, Kyle noticed how exhausted his wife looked in the flickering light of the citronella lamp, with Jason now asleep in her arms.

"What do you say we hit the hay?" he said.

She nodded and got up to follow Kyle inside. Looking across the ravine, she noticed the dancing lights of a campfire against a backdrop of trees. Awfully hot for a bonfire, she noted, as she shut the sliding glass door and embraced the air-conditioned atmosphere of their home.

Chapter 11

The Shaman's Apprentice

John Masters sat at his desk and stared at his calendar. Seeing that here were no appointments or other notes written on it made him smile. He hated commitments. The construction job he had worked since May was completed and his next job wasn't scheduled to begin until mid August, giving him at least three weeks off. He knew how much money he needed, and having reached that amount he decided not to pick up any odd jobs in the interim. Next to his calendar was a map. If his blank calendar made him smile, the map made him laugh outright. To him, it was the most beautiful wall decoration imaginable. It was a map of South America.

He first visited the South American continent while in the navy and fell in love with the atmosphere. Although he was never stationed there, the two weeks they ran maneuvers and the short leave they were granted convinced him that somehow he belonged there. Eventually, he returned and rented a small apartment near Rio Di Janeiro taking odd jobs to get by. His spare time was spent exploring the adjacent rain forest with his friend and guide, Gliner Rojas. Rojas, a native of Rio, operated a messenger service with his small plane. Trusted by the natives and accessible to South

American businessmen, his operation became a full time enterprise. The native tribesmen trusted him not to assault them with greedy, self-serving capitalists, and in return they granted him free passage to their villages. John soon became Rojas' partner, and in the process, an honorary member of the Mibiti tribe of Northwestern Brazil. The primitive village, found along a twisting Amazon tributary, became John's second home.

One day while John was in the village the tribesmen were startled by a loud scream. A young member of the tribe had fallen from a tree while collecting fruits and rendered unconscious. John ran to he boy and found him face down on the riverbank with no heartbeat or respiration. Instinctively, and without considering tribal customs, John knelt down beside the boy and commenced cardiopulmonary resuscitation. Within minutes, the boy began coughing, and minutes later, sat up, a bit dazed and sore but alive. After having been assumed dead by his family and fellow tribesmen, there he sat obviously alive and well.

Satisfied that the boy was all right, John turned to notice the entire tribe surrounding him in a semicircle, his back to the river. A hushed silence was broken only by the gasps as the village shaman,

Bitu, pushed through the crowd and hurried to the boy. He motioned

to the chief for an explanation. In such times, even the chief heeds

the shaman's demands. And especially in this case, because the boy

was none other than the chief's youngest son.

Instantly, John was overcome by a wave of nausea and dread.

He realized the possibility that by intervening with his life saving

efforts he had crossed the boundary of acceptable behavior. He had

treaded on the shaman's turf. He felt his legs wobble as the chief

and shaman discussed the matter.

Suddenly they concluded their conversation, and stride for

stride, approached John. The shaman stared powerfully into John's

eyes. He felt as if the shaman's stare penetrated his body with a

palpable energy. Then with silent, graceful power, the shaman

smiled, closed his eyes, and bowed his head to John. Instantly, the

tribesmen erupted in a joyful demonstration of celebration. John

was a hero, the shaman's newest apprentice.

By invitation, John decided to stay in the village indefinitely and

learn about medicinal plants with the shaman. On the days when

Rojas' plane could be heard in approach, the shaman would disappear into the forest. Rojas explained that the shaman distrusted visitors, and John was the first white man that the shaman agreed to accept as an apprentice. After about four weeks, the shaman announced to John that it was time to learn about the vine of the soul, or ayahuasca. Several times each month for a year or so, John would participate in the ayahuasca ceremonies. He was amazed at the variety of illnesses that the tea cured and the extent to which it preserved the health of the native tribesman.

Finally, after almost two years in the village, John decided he needed to return to the states and take care of some personal business. As he boarded Rojas' plane, the villagers stood waving and cheering, bidding John farewell and persuading him to return soon. With the shaman's permission John had brought a small sample of ayahuasca with him. The shaman had advised him to use it with a few of his good friends. Immediately, Craig and Bob came to mind. As John looked back at the waving villagers, growing tiny in the distance, he knew his return would be forthcoming.

Staring at his map, John knew the time had come. He wanted to share his ayahuasca experiences. It was a source of great pride and pleasure to have won the confidence of a powerful shaman, especially one who evaded outsiders so diligently. John was a privileged white man and it was an honor he did not take lightly. He wondered if his return would be met by the same enthusiasm and respect.

What John didn't know was that several Americans had attempted to infiltrate the village as he had done, only without the same success. Many years before, as the story is told, the shaman had warned of an assassination attempt within the Brazilian government. A missionary had heard about this ayahuasca prophecy, and fearing the political consequences, returned to the Brazilian Capital to warn the administration. When news reached President Rios he smiled, and acknowledging his reverence for the shaman's ayahuasca visions, refused to accept the prophecy. His assassination two days later stunned the South American continent, and the impact was felt as far as Washington D.C. Then President Carter was being pressured into action by various lobby groups to preserve the valuable rain forest lands. The global plundering of tropical forests was already impacting international economics, and Rios had found a powerful ally in the former peanut farmer turned President. Together, Carter and Rios were working toward a preservation agreement they hoped would be modeled in other regions of the world. The assassination of Rios all but obliterated the progress the two leaders had made.

The presidential successor to Rios, Juan Manuel, had no such preservation ideology. The here and now of the Brazilian economy called for slash and burn development, with it's delerterious effects on the environment. The CIA had attempted to investigate the so-called ayahuasca vision, which foretold the political upheaval. If they could incriminate Manuel in the as yet unsolved assassination of Rios, the U.S. Government could probably have him removed from power and restore conservation policies. Now with Ronald Reagan in power, the U.S. Government had even more pressing reasons to preserve the medicinal bounty of the rain forest--reasons that had to remain classified on the grounds of national security.

John Masters had no idea that the CIA was carefully watching his activities. As the only outsider permitted to enter the shaman's village he held the key to one of the CIA's greatest operations. As he packed his suitcase, the anticipation began to build. Shortly he would be back in the rain forest, deepening his involvement in a political and scientific mystery. Glancing in the kitchen to make sure his stove was off, he locked his door and headed for the airport.

Chapter 12

Craig's Dilemma

Telepathy is one of those controversial issues that has plagued modern science for years in much the same way that physiologists have struggled with the way that martial artists can pound a nail through solid oak with their foreheads--they have evidence that it happens, yet are at a loss to explain it. Of course, to a skilled martial artist, such feats are routine. To a telepath, gaining access to another person's mind is as natural as listening to a song on the radio. Hard core scientists dismiss such phenomena as anomalies, defying explanation and impossible to quantify.

Craig was no scientist. He was therefore very open minded about the messages he seemed to be receiving from his dream girl. He was intrigued by the fact that seven full days had passed since the ayahuasca visions, yet they remained as lucid as ever. Even vivid dreams tend to dissipate after several hours of wakefulness. His visions of Kelly were dancing around in his mind's eye. At first he thought it was simply an erotic fantasy. As the days passed, however, it became obvious that there was more to it than that. He actually felt that Kelly was speaking to him through her mind. But why Craig? And what the hell was she telling him? Unlike spoken language, the telepathic messages he received were more like feelings, emotions. They were vague but powerful. Kelly was trying to tell him she was in trouble. Or in a strange way, it was almost as if an intermediary was acting as messenger, delivering Kelly's message to Craig.

Craig felt he had two choices. Plan A involved painting his house and working on his lawn. Plan B involved getting to the bottom of the *Kelly* phenomenon, perhaps by participating in another ayahuasca ceremony. That's right. Drinking more ayahuasca. As if that was as easy as going to the grocery store for a half gallon of two percent. Even if he had a connection, he could imagine the response he'd get if he asked for a few cc's of ayahuasca. His only hope was John Masters, and he'd disappeared right after the weekend gathering.

Suddenly, Craig returned to planet earth. He inventoried the situation rationally. For starters, it wasn't such a good idea for a lawyer to experiment with exotic jungle drugs. In the " Just say no" society of Ronald Reagan, there was zero tolerance for drug use of any kind. Even if ayahuasca had yet to be identified and classified as a controlled substance, inevitably the U.S. Government would catch on. (In fact, harmine had just been placed on Schedule 1 status, rendering its use illegal under any circumstances.) Secondly, this fantasy about Kelly was destined for trouble. A little poking around revealed that she was happily married to a local doctor. Craig could see the headlines: *Drug Crazed Lawyer Arrested for Stalking Doctor's Wife.*

He looked disdainfully at the paint supplies he had just purchased for his house. *God,* he thought. *My life does need some excitement.* He began to feel exhilarated, albeit irrationally, with the idea that maybe, just maybe, he was destined to explore the realm of psychotropic drug use that had been man's birthright since time immemorial. No student of human history can ignore the significant role that plant drugs have played in the development of the human species. Suddenly, Craig realized that perhaps his ayahuasca experience was no accident. Perhaps he was chosen. He decided to get a hold of John and arrange for another session. He figured he had nothing to lose and everything to gain. Dialing John's number, there was still no answer. He remembered something one of his professors had said during a lecture at Michigan State: " Sometimes the need for discovery outweighs all other needs." Only now did he come to understand that statement. He was obsessed with exploring the drug-induced realms he had visited a week earlier.

He tried John again. No answer.

" I hope nothing's happened to him," Craig said aloud.

Chapter 13

The CIA

Special agent Peter Dressens approached the security entrance to

Wood Pharmaceuticals. Swiping his ID Card, then punching in his code word, the door unlocked and he entered quickly. Carrying a small vial of brownish liquid, he traversed the barren hallway to another locked steel door. Entering with a key, he found himself inside a state of the art pharmaceutical laboratory. There were several more CIA agents keeping a watchful eye.

The Special Biologics Division of Wood, Inc., was housed in an all brick, windowless building separated from the rest of the manufacturing plant by several hundred yards. The sprawling complex, home of the third largest pharmaceutical company in the world, covered two hundred acres of land and generated twelve billion dollars worth of pharmaceuticals a year. The Special Biologics Division was strictly a research facility and it had only one contract--The Central Intelligence Agency.

As early as 1962, the CIA had realized the importance of drug research, both in the areas of drug abuse and therapeutic applications. However, this facility researched neither of those areas. Their interest was in mind altering drugs, specifically hallucinogens. This project began in earnest with the assassination of President Rios in Brazil in 1977. There had been rumors of a prophetic, drug induced vision that was reported to the Brazilian Security office by a catholic missionary two days before the assassination. They felt that by locating the shaman and his unusual drugs they could possibly solve the murders. (Many of the CIA's missions were far from conservative.) They were totally unsuccessful in reaching the shaman. However, the locals were more than happy to supply them with samples of their own ayahuasca preparations in exchange for flashlights and clothing.

Using these secondary samples, the CIA needed a laboratory capable of analyzing unknown substances. Suprisingly, the government facilities in Virginia were not advanced enough. So the CIA took bids from the largest pharmaceutical houses in the United States to set up a high security facility dedicated entirely to CIA research. Wood, Inc. won the bid and constructed a separate lab for the research. It was here that the first government-sponsored research on ayahuasca was undertaken. Their initial results were startling.

The original tests done on rats were not remarkable. Microscopic neurologic examinations would not determine any brain function changes, perhaps because the rat brains were not developed enough to be affected by ayahuasca. The dog testing was more animated, with several of the dogs displaying unusual behavior. But, once again, brain slice examination of the sacrificed dogs didn't reveal any neurological changes. Then came the monkeys.

Given the estimated standard human dose, the monkeys fell into a trance-like state. EEG readings were off the scale, as if their brain waves were amplified. For hours the monkeys were observed responding to unseen stimuli, apparently being bombarded from within by images from the drug. Eventually, a few of the monkeys were sacrificed and their brains examined microscopically. The scientists couldn't believe their eyes.

The drugged brain tissue was compared against the control (non-drugged) brain tissue and the appearances were starkly different. Somehow, in a manner that still defies explanation, the ayahuasca induced massive growth of neuronal networks, in some cases in areas of the brain previously only marginally perfused. The ayahuasca had supercharged the monkey brains.

As exciting as the discoveries were, they led to little in the way of crime solving information. As the years passed and the Brazilian political arena quieted down, the research on ayahuasca became less critical. Several years later, however, it would once again become the focal point of a massive government research program. But this time, for an entirely different reason.

President Ronald Reagan had become one of the most popular U.S. Presidents of the post war era. The former actor and California Governor had won the love and respect of his countrymen, winning a second term in 1984. But it soon became apparent that the aging statesman was developing senile dementia, and increasingly it appeared to affect his performance. Years later, as an ex-president, he would be diagnosed with Alzheimer's Disease. However, at the height of his popularity and presidential power neither he nor his country could afford to allow an insidious disease to devour his judgment. It is one thing for a leader to be assassinated, but for a leader to lose his mental faculties, slowly over a long period of time, would erode his credibility and leadership abilities. No president had ever been declared unfit for office, and his cabinet didn't wish

for their leader to set a precedent.

Unfortunately, Alzheimer's is a disease of unknown etiology

with no cure. It wasn't until 1993 that Parke Davis released a drug

called tacrine, the first anti-Alzheimer's drug. In the meantime,

there was little hope. One prospect, Gingko Biloba, looked

promising but never materialized. Gingko was a tree that grew

naturally in the United States and it had been used for years as a folk

medicine to improve memory. Another trial drug, 5-

tetramethylaline, did appear to improve memory and cognitive skills,

but caused dangerous elevations in blood pressure. A secret

congressional committee agreed to fund research on any possible

treatment or cure for Alzheimer's at the Wood facility. The director

of the CIA was putting more and more pressure on the group at

Wood to come up with anything that would bolster at least the

President's image, if not his mental acuity.

Medicinal Chemist Roger Temple, Ph.D. had worked on the

original ayahuasca experiments at Wood. Daydreaming over a cup

of coffee one morning, he recalled the incredible results of neural growth in monkeys treated with ayahuasca. Within days a research team under Temple's leadership embarked on project R.O.N. (an acronym for Rejuvenation of Operational Neurons). Temple hoped to synthesize a compound with the neuronal boosting abilities found in ayahuasca, but without the psychotropic effects. Unfortunately, the researchers were using more of the ayahuasca samples than they originally intended. In other words, they needed more. Temple informed the CIA operatives that without more ayahuasca the research would come to a halt.

But there was more to it than that. Over the years, several field agents had collected dozens of samples from all over South America. As was to be expected, each sample was slightly different. Looking at his research notes, Temple concluded that the most active sample had been labeled 8RD12. Calling up the materials listing on his computer screen, he looked for the source of the sample that he needed so badly.

MATERIALS INCODED PROJECT R.O.N.

BETA CARBOLINE SAMPLES

14TF01   BINITA,
PERU

14LF07
SUBORA, PERU

17FG05   RIO
VAUPES, BRAZIL

18FG07   RIO
VAUPES, BRAZIL

81RD12   MIBITI
TRIBE, BRAZIL

10BN02
MANBY, PERU

INQUIRY: CONTACT SOURCE 81RD12

REPLY: SHAMAN NEVER FOUND

Apparently, the field operatives were able to follow an

American they believed to be smuggling ayahuasca into the states.

Before long, they would trace the brown tea to a kitchen table in a

house belonging to an Ohio lawyer. They would soon have their

sample and Temple's research could resume.

Chapter 14

The Pediatrician

Kelly awoke one morning from a vivid, confusing dream.

Crippled over with pain, she was met by her neighbor, the young

lawyer, on a wooded hillside.   She didn't recognize the location, as

it was completely alien terrain. The lawyer, whose name she would

later learn was Craig, coerced her to drink a strange liquid from an even stranger ceramic bowl. Craig had convinced her that the liquid would purge her system of the cause of her pain.

She sat up in bed. It was nine-fifteen and Kyle was already gone. Collecting her thoughts, she remembered that Jason had an appointment with the pediatrician that morning. Dr. Moorehead preferred that all nursing babies be seen on a monthly basis for the first six months. Kelly didn't mind, as long as Dr. Moorehead continued to be supportive of breast feeding Many young mothers abandon breast milk when their babies become colicky. Kelly wanted to stick it out, preferably with her doctor's approval.

Shaking off her disturbing dream, Kelly bathed with Jason and prepared for their late morning appointment. She'd decided to pick up sandwiches at Kyle's favorite delicatessen and surprise him for lunch. Dr. Moorehead's office was a half-hour's drive across town. Jason slept the whole way. Kelly had intentionally asked for the last appointment before lunch so it would coincide with Kyle's break when they finished at the doctor's office.

After a brief wait, they were ushered into a small examination room, decorated sparsely with Disney characters. No matter how hard physicians try, there's no way to disguise a medical facility. Jason was groggily waking up, and complained loudly when Kelly didn't produce his favorite food source--her breast. She figured she would nurse him in the van when they finished.

Dr. Moorehead entered with a quick knock. He was fifty-two and looked it. He smiled as he reached out for Jason's hand, his bald head shining as he bent over. He was from the old school of medicine, which taught that there was no room for arrogance. He was usually receptive to the parent's viewpoint, and with Kelly being a physician's spouse he gave her even more respect.

Unlike most pediatricians, he preferred measuring and weighing the babies himself. After entering the numbers, he set down his clipboard and faced Kelly.

" Any problems?" he asked with a smile.

" Just the usual. We're hoping this crying will stop soon."

" Still no cow's milk or wheat, right?"

" Yep. What I wouldn't do for a double cheese pizza right now!" Kelly laughed. For many nursing babies, the mother's diet can profoundly affect their little bellies. In most cases dairy is the

offending party. But some mothers need to eliminate wheat products

as well. Understandably, with the typical North American diet,

there's little left to eat after you've cut out everything with milk or

wheat. It's been a struggle for Kelly.

Moorehead turned suddenly serious. " I'd like to discuss this in

detail with Kyle as well, but I feel it may be time to do a scope. For

some reason, I'm not convinced that this is colic."

Suddenly, Kelly doubled over in pain.

" Hey, you all right?" Moorehead rushed over.

" Yeah, it's going away." Kelly looked up with tears in her

eyes.

" I take it that's happened before."

" Unfortunately."

" Ulcer?"

" Can't find it if it's there," she said.

Moorehead couldn't hide his concerned look. Kelly looked at him curiously. Cocking her head as she looked at him, she pressed him. " You don't think there's a relationship?" Suddenly the whole picture had changed. Could she have passed a medical problem to her child congenitally?

" I'll have to do some research. In the meantime, I'd like you to keep a diary. List everything you eat, I mean everything, and keep track of those attacks. Also, try to monitor his crying spells. We might possibly find a relationship if we have enough data." He paused and shifted uncomfortably on his stool. Kelly could tell he was holding something back.

" What is it?" She asked.

" Kyle," he hesitated. " What does he make of this?"

" That's how we met. He was my doctor in the hospital. But he's never been able to diagnose a ..." she stopped. " He thinks my pains have stopped." She looked down at her feet. Jason was fast asleep on her shoulder. Looking up again she continued. " I don't want Kyle to worry about me. He's got too much going on right now."

" I don't want to step on his toes," Moorehead said. " But I'd like you to consider pursuing your condition. I have a hunch we've been missing something."

" Kyle's real funny about my seeing other doctors. He even does my annual Pap smear. If he could fit contact lenses, he would."

" Talk to him. Or have him call me. I'm not questioning his skills. We can, I should say we need, to work together," he said with sincerity.

" I agree," Kelly said as she stood. " I'll talk to him. Thank you, doctor."

He winked and nodded. " Don't despair. 'Incurable' is not a word in my vocabulary."

Kelly was both exhilarated and frightened. If Moorehead's hunch was right, Jason may have inherited her abdominal problems. She wondered how Kyle would react to Moorehead's suggestion that they pursue Kelly's problems. Picking up their lunches, she decided not to mention anything until later that night.

Entering the Professional Building East, she walked down the hallway to Kyle's office. He was just finishing up with his last morning appointment.

" There's my big boy." He held out his arms to Jason, who smiled at his dad. " Did you have to go the baby doctor today?"

" Yes, he did and everything 's fine." Kelly hated lying. She looked at Jason to avoid eye contact with her husband. " I brought you corned beef, is that OK?"

" Great. Thank you." He kissed her on the cheek and tasted salt. He looked at Kelly's eyes and noticed they were pooling with tears. Unable to hold back, she sat down and cried uncontrollably. Taking the cue, Jason joined in.

Chapter 15

The Shaman

It is no great secret that to the arrogant, modern medical establishment, a shaman of the virginal rain forest is no more of a healer than a two-year-old with a toy stethoscope. Yet, as twentieth century physicians poison their patients with progressively more and more toxic chemicals, the primitive medicine men serve their people well though the use of pharmacologically active plants with few side effects. And while the revered medical doctor had begun to lose the trust and respectability he once enjoyed, the shamans continue inspiring complete reverence from those that they serve. And it is this reverence that contributes to the healing powers of the medicine men, just as the lack of respect for a medical doctor can undermine the healing process completely.

Bitu is renowned throughout the region as a powerful shaman, perhaps for no other reason besides his age. Although shamanism exists on all corners of the globe, important cultural differences make it difficult to universally define their creed. One aspect of shamanism common to all cultures is the belief in the *other worlds* and the shaman's role as an intermediary between the worlds. In fact, most shamans attain their status as a direct result of a spectacular journey to another world in connection with an initiation crisis, which often mimics madness. Subsequent journeys can occur spontaneously, or more frequently, they are catalyzed by the consumption of mind-altering drugs. In either case, the journey to the other world is usually associated with a gain of knowledge usually in conjunction with the healing of a sick member of the tribe.

The journey is often a vividly terrifying experience that can happen to anyone, anytime. It is believed that many who are not prepared for the experience do not survive. Those that do, and have subsequent journeys, find their role in the tribe changes. They become responsible for the interplay between the tribe and the spirits of the other sphere. Through their apprenticeship to another shaman, they learn to identify and use medicinal plants. Throughout the domain of shamans worldwide there are plants that are considered sacred. The American southwest and Mexico have Peyote (Lophophora Williamsii) and "Magic Mushrooms (Psylocibe species), Asian shamans have fly agaric (amanita muscaria), medieval Europeans had the nightshades (mandrake, henbane) and the list goes on.

Perhaps the most intriguing of the vision inducing drugs is ayahuasca from the Amazon. It is unique in that it is the only sacred plant drug that is actually a combination of different plant drugs. As researchers in modern laboratories began to study the brew, it became obvious that not only was the chemistry difficult to ascertain, the actual plants used in the preparation were not known in their entirety. Several ethnobotanical researchers have made some progress in identifying the plants used most commonly but there are still several plant ingredients that remain mysteriously unknown. Legends say that the soul of the vine itself pointed out to the ancient shamans which plants to mix to prepare the tea. Once ingested, ayahuasca's other unique characteristic emerges--that of triggering a communal mind or telepathy. It is precisely this bizarre effect that was impacting the lives of Craig and Kelly. John Masters was the emissary between them and the shaman's curative vine.

John was still confused by the whole series of events. He was hoping this trip would answer his questions. As he boarded Rojas' plane and viewed the familiar velvety green canopy below, he began to wonder what he'd gotten his friend and his friend's neighbor into.

Learning about medicinal plants from the shaman and experiencing the ayahuasca visions were enviable pursuits, but he'd never planned on getting more people involved. However, he firmly believed that Craig and Kelly were somehow involved and John felt obligated to unravel the mystery of Craig's telepathic connection to Kelly. As the plane droned onward toward the unspoiled village, John smiled to himself. If nothing else, it was all a good excuse to get back.

The plane approached the dirt runway, twisting left and right for position. John could see several natives waiting already, having heard the unmistakable sounds of airplane engines. He was always grateful for the escort, as it was not easy to traverse the jungle alone.

Waving goodbye to Rojas, John turned to his friends. They bowed in reverence. John was pleased that his apprenticeship was still accepted. Reaching into his bag, he produced two mini flashlights as gifts to the men who grabbed his other supplies. Silently, they left the barren airstrip and entered the forest.

John always seemed to forget how far any given destination was in the forest. For the natives, a two-hour walk was routine. For John, a two-hour walk on a paved sidewalk was a rigorous undertaking, let alone through dense jungle trails. He made the journey more pleasant by seeking out some of the plants that Bitu had taught him about. He found it curious that the other members of the tribe could do little in the way of plant identification. In some cases, two members would give conflicting information on a plant's identity or possible medicinal use. John suspected that there was probably a secretive motive behind their supposed ignorance. After finding only a few recognizable species, John grew tired of searching and focused on the trail, which in many spots was little more than a slim space between thick branches.

Some two hours later John could detect the familiar and welcome aroma of campfires. He was surprised to find the village practically abandoned, except for the women who tended the children and fires. The women in the tribe were extremely shy towards John, which was fortunate because any sign of flirtation

would be disastrous. Arriving at his customary hut, John busied

himself with unpacking and setting up mosquito netting. Resting on

his straw mat, he sized up his plan of action. For the first time since

his involvement with the shaman, John had a specific agenda. Not

willing to go along with a random tag along approach, he was unsure

of how to approach Bitu with the Craig and Kelly story. Just as he

began to doze off, as he so often did when faced with a major

dilemma, Yaru, the chief's twenty year old nephew, entered his hut

with a couple of potato like vegetables and a bowl of cassava beer.

John was informed that the other men were hunting and would

probably not return until daybreak, if not longer. Thanking Yaru,

John eagerly consumed his meal, even drinking the cassava beer.

When John learned how cassava was fermented--saliva enzymes

donated by the women triggered the fermentation of manioc--he was

turned off. The taste grew on him after awhile, though, and soon he

found himself craving it. After a brief and solitary stroll around the

village to digest his meal, John made his way back to his hut and the safety of the mosquito net. Soon he was enveloped by nightfall and sleep.

John was awakened by the heat of the morning. Gathering his senses, he stepped out of his hut and approached Yaru, who was repairing a nearby hut. As John neared the chief's nephew, with whom he felt comfortably friendly, he rehearsed in his mind the language of the tribe. On several occasions he had embarrassed, even enraged, some of the tribe with his poorly selected words. It turned out that he didn't need words this time.

Before he could get within speaking distance, Yaru made a crisp pointing gesture toward Bitu's hut. John nodded with understanding. Apparently, the shaman had instructed Yaru to guide John to him upon awakening. John obeyed and changed course toward the peripheral hut of Bitu.

John had not fully assessed his relationship with the powerful shaman. It was not friendship or even paternalism. Obviously, there was some motive on the shaman's part to accept this stranger as an apprentice. John hoped that when he found out he wouldn't regret it. He was about to learn the answer.

Approaching Bitu's hut quietly, John searched for signs of activity. There were none. Before he could decide the appropriate manner with which to announce his arrival, Bitu beckoned him inside. Entering the sparsely furnished hut, Bitu silently motioned for John to sit. He smiled.

"I'm glad you've returned." Bitu stated.

"I thank you for having me." John smiled back, a bit uncomfortably.

"You have a problem?" Asked the shaman.

It took John off guard. *How did he know?*

"Yes. With my friends." Replied John rather vaguely.

"There is a sickness with your friend?"

John explained Craig's vision and the reaction he had to seeing Kelly that morning of the walk. He still wasn't sure himself what to say about it.

"It is time for you to journey. We have reason to go to her and help. There is a baby?"

John did remember that Kelly had a baby with her. "Yes. But …"

"We heal baby and mother. Put your friend at ease. We travel to her tonight."

There was strength in Bitu's words. He somehow knew John's main reason for coming.

"You have something from your friend?" asked the shaman.

John looked puzzled.

Bitu reached out his hand. "You have something your friend gave you, something to guide us to him?"

John was totally confused. Something from Craig? He reached into his pocket and pulled out a pocketknife Craig had given him. "Like this?"

Bitu grabbed the knife. "This will show us the way. You sit." With that, Bitu stood and reached for a gourd next to his straw mat. It was ayahuasca. "Tonight we visit your friends."

John could not describe his feelings at that moment. He was about to embark on his first attempt at soul flight. Fear and excitement changed to anticipation as Bitu passed him the gourd.

Chapter 16

Dr. Ferguson's Bad Day

By the time Cathy Clarke RN reached room 519, the patient was barely breathing. Twenty-seven year old Bill Nelson had been admitted two days ago for abdominal pain and was currently under observation. The blood discovered in Nelson's stool was noted in the chart as possible hemorrhoids, unrelated to his abdominal pain. Unfortunately, he was suffering from an acute attack of ulcerative colitis, with toxins from the affected intestinal wall invading his bloodstream. He was in shock as Nurse Clarke took his temperature--104 degrees. She checked his chart to notify the last physician on rounds. Kyle Ferguson.

Ferguson had just added the sugar to his first cup of coffee when his beeper went off. Tossing an ice cube in his mug to facilitate

quick consumption, he dialed the nursing station indicated on his
beeper.

" Five west," replied the ward clerk.

" This is Dr. Ferguson, returning a page," he said

" Patient in 519 went into shock with temp 104."

" Right there." Setting his mug down, Kyle raced for the
elevator. Trying to remember room 519 he drew a blank. Rubbing
his eyes to remove the residue from another sleepless night, Kyle
hoped he looked better than he felt. Entering 519, he found a
critically ill patient that seemed stable just last night during his final
rounds. The nurses looked up, awaiting instructions.

" Vitals?" He asked, grabbing the chart.

" BP 90/60, temp 104, respiration 40, rectal bleeding."

Kyle could see without lifting the bedsheets that there was
horrific blood loss. " Call OR. He needs prepped. *Now*." he
bellowed. Delaying the surgical consult upon admission now
loomed as a major blunder. He knew this patient was in grave
danger. He wanted to hide somewhere.

" Page me if there's any status info," he said. " I'll be in my office."

Returning to his office, Kyle found a drug rep waiting at his door, with his three-piece suit, black leather briefcase and an obnoxious smile

" Hi. Bill Jackson with Wood Pharmaceuticals. We had an appointment?" he said with his salesmanlike pitch. " Is this still a good time?"

Kyle groaned to himself. There was never a good time to deal with drug reps. Unfortunately, it was usually the easiest way to keep up with the latest developments in the drug industry. Although obviously biased, the drug reps did provide a wealth of information about drug therapies. After listening to a monologue, Kyle showed the rep to the door, went back to his desk, kicked up his feet and replayed in his mind the diagnostic blunder responsible for Bill Nelson's condition.

He awoke to a knock on his door. He'd been asleep over an hour. Straightening his tie and running his fingers through his hair, he opened the door. Dr. Herbert Melton greeted him. Melton was chief of staff and appeared to be in a not so good mood. Kyle tried hard to disguise the fact that he'd been fast asleep minutes ago.

"Dr. Melton. Come in please." Kyle said as enthusiastically as possible.

Melton entered Kyle's office and, instead of sitting down, milled about for a few minutes, glancing at Kyle's stacks of charts and medical books strewn about. Finally he stood in front of one of the chairs setting opposite Kyle's desk.

"Please sit," said Kyle. "To what do I owe the pleasure?" he asked, hiding sarcasm.

"Kyle, we've known each other a long time," began Melton "You're one of the brightest internists we've had here in some time." He paused. Kyle could tell the shit was about to hit the fan.

"Is there a problem?" Kyle asked.

"That's what I wanted to ask you. Is everything all right in your life? Any problems at home you'd like to discuss?"

Kyle took a deep breath. "Is this about Bill Nelson?" He then realized that OR had not reported on Nelson's condition--unless he'd slept through the page . . .

"He died on the table. Didn't they call you?"

"No!" Kyle sounded surprised. He was.

"Look Kyle. We're not in the practice of hounding every doctor who loses a patient. Frankly, we're not sure anyone could have diagnosed the severity of Nelson's ulcerative condition." He stood up and paced behind the chair. "No. It's other complaints we've had, from nursing and other doctors. You seem to be unfocused, lax."

Kyle was stunned by the accusation. True, there were days when he felt unmotivated, but he wasn't aware that fellow staffers had noticed. His voice wavered. "Complaints? What kind?"

"Look Kyle. This is an informal visit. There's a lot of concern for your well being, that's all."

Melton had both hands on the back of his chair, staring right at Kyle.

"I guess Jason's taken more out of me than I thought," admitted Kyle.

"Still keeping you up all night?" Melton asked, a little more sympathetically.

"We're stumped. Moorehead is too," said Kyle, referring to the pediatrician.

"Colic?"

"That's what we thought. But it's certainly not typical. I'm beginning to wonder."

"Well, if there's anything we can do, don't hesitate," said Melton with sincerity. "Look to friends and colleagues for support, understand?"

Kyle nodded. "Thank you. I will."

"Good. Now I'll let you get back to work."

Kyle stood in the doorway watching Melton trod back down the hall. Maybe he did need help. He was jolted from his reverie by the intercom.

"Dr. Ferguson?"

"This is Ferguson."

"Janet Wright, Administration."

"What can I do for you?" asked Kyle.

"State Inspectors are in the building. Need your charts. Up to date, if possible."

"What do you mean?"

"State regs. Protocols."

"I'm not sure my charts are caught up." Kyle was nervous. All state-funded hospitals were required to maintain stringent guidelines for their record keeping and chart maintenance. Kyle was somewhat behind with his paperwork, and the timing couldn't have been worse. He didn't want to be the doctor responsible for an accreditation infraction. It could make his life miserable. "How long do I have?" he asked.

"They'll probably be up to your unit by tomorrow noon."

"All right. Thanks for the warning." Kyle looked at his watch. It was already six o'clock. He then looked at his desk, piled high with charts. It would take him all night to get caught up. He picked up his empty coffee cup and decided he'd better call Kelly.

"Hello?"

"Hi babe." He as already tired.

"Hi. What's wrong?"

He always marveled at how she could read his voice. Giving her the bad news, he apologized.

"I'm sorry. Kiss Jason for me. And call me in the morning, make sure I'm still alive." He tried to sound cheerful.

"You want me to come down and help?"

"Nah. Just relax. There's not much anyone can do," he said.

"OK. Don't forget to eat. I love you."

"I love you too. Pleasant dreams." Kyle hung up, gathered his strength and pulled the first chart off the stack. It was sure to be a long, long night.

Chapter 17

Nightmare

After a quick dinner, Kelly decided to take a bath with Jason. It had been a long time since she'd last stayed home alone, and certainly the first time since having Jason. She wanted to get the bathing and other bedtime chores over with early. The bath seemed to soothe Jason a little, but did nothing for her. For some reason, she had a strange feeling that it was going to be a long night, and it would take more than a long bath to erase her anxiety. At first, she thought she'd be more comfortable sleeping with Jason on the couch in front of the television set. But after a few minutes, she realized that her back would feel like it had been struck repeatedly with a sledgehammer so she locked up and headed for the bedroom.

Since childhood, she'd always had the problem of feeling watched when alone in a dark room. Tonight was no exception, perhaps even worse. Climbing into bed, she assumed her customary nursing position, on her side with Jason at her breast. In that position it was virtually impossible to read so she flipped on the TV. At some point during the weather report Jason fell asleep but, being a little on edge still, she stayed up and started watching the Tonight Show. Setting the sleep timer for thirty minutes, she didn't make it through the monologue.

What happened next will never exactly be known, other than the sheer terror that overcame the young mother. It had to be a dream. Yet it was so real that Kelly would forever be unable to sleep alone in that house again. Although many dreams seem to be incredibly realistic, Kelly had never experienced anything like this. She was able to watch Jason asleep, watch the clock advance, and to know what pajamas she was wearing, all the while asleep in a dream. She knew it had to be a dream--actually a nightmare. How else could she explain the presence of a primitive medicine man hovering over her in bed examining her abdomen? The old shaman was wearing a red loincloth, a neckful of beads and face paint as he straddled her knees and leaned over her stomach. She would feel his hands as they explored her entire abdominal region. As he worked his way down

to her pajama bottoms, she closed her eyes and braced for the worst.

Unable to scream, she reopened her eyes. The shaman was still

there, now waving his hands over her body. He had not touched her

in a violating manner. All she could feel now was an unusual

warmth that emanated from the palms of his hands. She cocked her

head to make sure Jason was all right. He hadn't budged. But while

she was glancing at her baby, out of the corner of her eye in the cold

darkness of the bedroom she caught a fleeting glimpse of what

appeared to be another figure looking at her. Closing her eyes again

she tried to will herself to sleep, to no avail. She opened her eyes in

horror, unable to move, as the shaman examined Jason with

surprising gentleness. At one point Jason opened his eyes and stared

intently at the strange man holding him. Kelly waited for the

requisite screaming, but it never came. Instead Jason allowed the

shaman to gently lay him back down on the bed where he promptly

fell back asleep.

Once again, the shaman's attention turned to Kelly. As his

hands came down slowly toward her head, she again tried in vain to scream. Preparing for the assault, she was instead subjected to a powerful sensation which caused her eyelids to shut tightly. She found with horror that she was unable to reopen them. After what seemed like a kaleidoscope of light and color, accompanied by warm gusts of air surrounding the bed, she discovered that she could now open her eyes, and finally, scream.

Down the street, Craig awoke to go to the bathroom in the middle of the night. Too tired to stand, he sat on the toilet to urinate, cursing the last beer he had before bed that caused the rude awakening. He heard what he thought was a scream. Then silence. Then, unmistakably, another scream in the distance. Working his way to a bedroom window, he marveled at the surrealistic appearance of the neighborhood courtesy of a nearly full moon and clear skies. The serenity was annihilated by the emergence of a screaming woman, running with her baby. Clad only in pajamas, she was heading toward the street. Craig couldn't believe his eyes. It was her!

Bounding downstairs with unlikely grace for a man who was dead asleep minutes before, he bolted for the front door and headed for the screams.

"Hey! What's' going on?" he screamed.

"Oh my god!" Kelly screamed as she headed for the friendly voice. "Help me!"

Craig was looking around for the cause for the commotion. Seeing nothing, he concentrated his gaze on Kelly as she closed the gap. If the moon had enhanced the beauty of the landscape, he couldn't describe the effect it had on Kelly's appearance. Accentuating her near perfect figure and the natural beauty of her face, the moonlit scene augmented the fear in her eyes. Craig opened his arms and Kelly accepted the offer, sandwiching a now screaming Jason between them. For several minutes, in the safety of Craig's hug, Kelly sobbed uncontrollably. She didn't want to budge.

"Hey, come on." Craig tried to calm her as he brushed her hair from her teary eyes. "Tell me what's wrong. You're safe now."

"A man. A weirdo in by bedroom. I thought it was a dream, but
. . ."

Craig thought for a moment, then asked, "Where's your
husband. Is he OK?"

Kelly nodded. "He's at work. Then all this happened." She
planted a kiss on Jason's forehead. "What did he want from me?"

"Are you sure this wasn't a nightmare?" Craig began to wonder
what nightmare could have caused such fear.

"I don't know, I just . . ." she started crying again.

Craig began to lead her towards his house. "Do you want to call
the police or your husband?"

The suddenness of Craig's question suddenly brought Kelly
back from the terror of the night. Forget the police, she thought.
What would she tell them? That she couldn't handle a bad dream?
And Kyle. She knew he wouldn't be able to stay at work knowing
what went on and she didn't want to burden him with that. She
looked at Craig. Somewhat handsome, even with a pillow head from
sleep, with a well-trimmed beard, he looked like he was someone's

boyfriend, but not husband. For some reason he just looked like a bachelor. She recalled the morning their eyes met and the realization suddenly hit that she had finally met this young lawyer.

"Is it all right if we stay for a few minutes?" she asked vulnerably.

"You can stay all night if you like. Just excuse the mess."

Guiding them into his family room, he offered her his recliner, the same one that he had occupied during his ayahuasca trip. With unabashed forwardness, she lifted her pajama blouse and brought Jason to her breast. Looking up, she noticed Craig's embarrassed expression.

"Oh. I'm sorry. I'm just so used to it," she said.

"No problem." Craig still could not believe what was going on. "When you're ready, I can go back and search your house for you." He surprised himself with his boldness. Kelly was debunking the single man's myth--that a woman lost her youthful, sexy appearance after giving birth.

"Would you?" She paused. "But you probably need to get back to sleep."

"I'm fine. Really. Just want to help." He was convinced that Kelly had experienced a lucid nightmare. A quick inspection of her house would settle the issue. Suddenly, a look of shock overpowered Kelly's face.

"What is it?" Craig moved closer.

"There was another man in my room. Not a weirdo like the one on my bed." She muttered calmly.

"What did he look like?"

She paused, looking intently at Craig. Finally she spoke flatly, as if in a trance. "It was your friend. The tall one with the pony tail."

Chapter 18

Craig and Kelly

Not surprisingly, Craig found it hard to concentrate on the mundane affairs of the legal profession the day after the Kelly incident. Once she had calmed down, they had returned to the Ferguson house. Craig inspected every room and it was determined that no intruders were present. In fact it looked like no intruders had ever been present. Even Kelly's jewelry, including a valuable tennis bracelet, was still on the nightstand as she'd left them. Certainly a robber or rapist would have snatched up such a conspicuously valuable diamond bracelet without a thought. After thanking him profusely Kelly showed Craig to the door and he departed, exhausted but happy to have been able to help.

Once home, even though it was after three in the morning, Craig could not sleep. The allegation that John had been in Kelly's bedroom stuck in his mind. John had mentioned the possibility of soul flight in which a body could materialize in a different geographical region while under the influence of ayahuasca, but Craig was always skeptical. What would John want with Kelly,

anyway? Finally, around five, Craig was able to put the mystery
aside and fall asleep.

After meeting with a few of his clients, Craig decided to try
reaching John again, to no avail. Driving himself crazy with the
event, Craig began pacing his small office a few steps in each
direction. Rationally, there were only two possibilities. The most
likely, and the one that Craig believed to be the case, was the
nightmare explanation. Kelly had seen John's face that morning
they walked the neighborhood enough to incorporate it into a dream.
Another possibility was that there were intruders in the house, one
resembling John, who were somehow spooked and decided to exit
before getting caught.

But what if there was a third explanation? Could John have
projected himself along with Bitu? And if so, why? Craig realized
that John might in fact be in Brazil. He decided to call the only
person he could think of to talk about this mystery--Bob Timmons.
Craig hadn't seen Bob since they drank the tea. He wasn't sure how
Bob felt about the whole experience, but he might be able to

rationalize the situation. Searching his wallet for Bob's number, Craig rested the phone on his shoulder and dialed.

"Blackburn Products," answered the cheerful receptionist.

"Bob Timmons, please," Craig asked.

"I'll ring."

After six rings Craig almost gave up, when Bob answered.

"Bob Timmons."

"Hi guy. How's it going?"

"Hi Craig. Haven't talked to you since that weekend."

"Yeah, are you recovered yet?"

"No problem. Something to tell the kids someday. Can you hold on?"

"Sure," Craig said. He would hear Bob cupping his hand over the mouthpiece and conversing with a co-worker. He was an industrial designer for a plastic manufacturer.

"Sorry. Yeah, that was an experience. I tried to call John but he's never around."

"Me too. I think he's in Brazil, actually," said Craig.

"Yeah? Probably drinking tea right now."

"I had a weird experience last night," began Craig. He proceeded to tell Bob all about the night before, with close attention to details. When he finished there was silence at the other end.

"Bob? Hello?" he asked.

"Craig, that's kind of weird," was all Bob could say. "What do you mean, John was in this lady's bedroom?"

"That's what she said. I didn't give it much credence either. Then I remembered what John had said about traveling. You know, actually materializing in another place while on the drug." Craig was carefully picking out his words.

"Are you talking about astral projection?"

"Kind of. I don't know. All I can tell you is that Kelly was scared shitless."

"So now you're on a first name basis with her, eh?" Bob was ribbing him. "I think she's just after you."

"Yeah. She's ready to ditch her doctor hubby for me. C'mon. I'm serious. I mean, do you think it's at all possible? You're the one telling us to keep an open mind all the time." Craig pleaded.

Bob paused, then continued in a more serious tone. "There have always been references to soul flight. There's some very interesting research going on, but I don't think anyone's ever accomplished it during a controlled experiment."

"I wish we could get a hold of John," sighed Craig. "I wonder when he'll be back?"

"I don't know," said Bob. " But when he does, we can run an experiment of our own."

"You want to try it again?" asked Craig.

"For sure. I'll be ready this time." He started laughing. "Maybe I'll travel to what's her name's bedroom!"

"Very funny. If you were there last night you'd realize this was no joke."

"I know. I'm serious. I'd like to set up an experiment."

"Like what?" asked Craig.

"Well, something simple, easy to prove. Like setting up a recognizable item in my office here and having you or John travel here to find out what is," Bob said.

There was silence. "Craig?"

"I just thought of something. I wonder if John could describe anything in Kelly's bedroom."

"I don't think Kelly's husband would be happy to hear any of this," laughed Bob.

"No! You know what I mean. I looked over that room carefully. If John was there we should have some common, recognizable memories of some of the things in that room."

"Well there's only one way to find out," Bob said, referring to John. "He'll be able to solve this mystery right off."

"I guess," countered Craig.

"Why the doubt?" asked Bob.

"Come on, Bob. What if he *can* identify an item or two in that room? Could that really prove that he *traveled* here from Brazil? And that we could do it too?"

"Remember, you need to have an open mind."

"Shut up, you asshole." They both laughed. "What about this Kelly, anyway?" Craig changed the subject. "What has she got to do with all of this?"

"Maybe John can explain that too."

"Yeah. Maybe. Let me know when you hear from him."

"Ditto. Talk to you later," Bob said.

As Craig hung up, he found himself obsessed with this event. Soul flight? And what did Kelly have to do with Craig and his friends? He knew the answer would materialize soon. And when it did, he wanted to be prepared.

Chapter 19

John Returns With the Shaman's Plan

John Masters could never remember being so restless on an airplane. Usually, he was anything but anxious to return to the states after visiting Brazil. But this time was different. His apprenticeship with Bitu had taken a dramatic turn. No longer was their association casual, the lessons random. For the first time in his life John had a true mission. He knew now why a shaman in the Amazon was so anxious to reveal his secrets to an American construction worker. John had always believed in someday realizing what meaningful goals he would pursue. Now that such a goal was revealed to him, he was entangled in a confusing web of emotions. Fear, confusion, ecstasy, skepticism, and most of all, excitement. He had never felt so alive, so sure of his place in the universe.

Five rows back, in the aisle seat, agent Peter Dressens was quite sure of John Master's place in the universe- Row 18, seat 5, to be exact, on route to Port Columbus International Airport. Upon landing, he would direct security to search John's bags, and upon finding the ayahuasca, would arrest him. He smiled inside, maintaining his stoic exterior. He lived for successful missions.

John did not bring any ayahuasca with him. There was simply not enough time for him to assist Bitu in preparing a batch for the road. Bitu agreed that once a batch was ready he would summon Rojas who could ship it to John directly. Without any contraband, there was no reasonable need for Dressens to detain John. He knew that if he moved in at the wrong time, he would jeopardize any further opportunity to procure the special ayahuasca. His surveillance would have to continue.

John went straight home from the airport. Immediately upon entering his apartment he saw his answering machine lit up like a

Christmas tree. Normally, he would have ignored it and plowed into bed, but he was too stimulated from his trip to think about sleeping. He pressed the play button on his machine, and smiled upon hearing both Craig and Bob's messages. *Wait until they hear.*

The room was silent. After Craig had relived his night with Kelly, he waited for John's response. John simply stood and began pacing the floor of Craig's family room. He was trying to figure out where to begin, although he'd rehearsed his story several times in his head. It wasn't that he didn't believe it, it was more a case of trying to simplify a very complicated situation. He began slowly.

"We were there that night," he said, referring to Kelly's bedroom. "Bitu took me there to confirm his story."

"What story?" asked a bewildered Craig.

"I'm not sure where to begin," said John as he combed his fingers through his hair. "But here goes."

Bob and Craig looked at each other as John began. Several years ago, according to John, Bitu encountered an ethnobotanist studying plants in his region. Ethnobotanists are botanists who specialize in studying plant use by native peoples, usually for medicinal purposes. Apparently Bitu was impressed by the scientist's sincerity. Rather than prodding him for information, he merely wanted to express his concerns for the ecology of the rain forest. He made a plea to Bitu to allow botanists into the region to study plant drugs and his reasoning was sensible. According to the botanist, William Rogers, a single plant drug that proved to be a life saving medicine or cure would generate a great deal of capital which in turn could be used to combat the destruction of the forest by indiscriminate developers. In other words, the discovery of a useful drug would ensure the preservation of the rain forest. There would be more money to be made by saving the vegetation and carefully cultivating the medicinal plants than could be made through commercial development, which ravaged the environment. As Bitu witnessed the encroachment of civilization in his sacred forest, the botanist's plea became even more pertinent. The aging shaman realized the importance of discovering an appropriate use for one of the many of the plant drugs in his pharmacopeon.

He had to turn no further than the sacred vine for the answer. During an ayahuasca session he was "told" by the vine that his apprentice, John, was in the vicinity of a sick child and mother whose illness would provide the answer. Bitu gave John a bottle of the tea and purposefully instructed John to give some to his friends who could pinpoint the source of Bitu's message. It was Craig, whose visions of Kelly provided the solution. His encounter with Kelly held the answer. Bitu needed John to guide him, and John obliged not realizing yet what it was all about. Guided by the energy in the pocketknife that was given to him by Craig, Bitu was able to travel to the source of the disturbance, with John in tow.

John paused. Craig and Bob had to sit in silence listening to the story. Craig began to speak, but John held up his hand for silence.

" Let me tell you the whole story, then you can fire away, OK?" said John. Craig nodded. Although the details were sketchy, John recounted his soul flight experience. He felt himself levitate soon after drinking the tea, and felt himself being propelled along with Bitu into a whirlwind of extreme motion. It was similar in effect to the sensation of falling so common in dreams, yet this was more directional. The next thing he knew, he was in a strange bedroom, with Bitu standing over the bed. He watched in this dreamlike state as Bitu performed his diagnostic examination of Kelly. Satisfied with the results, he seemingly pulled John with him, reversing the travel . John awoke on the ground, next to the campfire. Bitu then explained the whole event.

"What he told me about Kelly will probably end up in the medical journals very soon," he continued. According to Bitu, Kelly and her baby, along with a good percentage of the general population, were infected with an unusual parasite, not yet known to western science. In effect, Kelly had been infected years ago and had unwittingly passed the parasite transplacentally to Jason. It was causing her abdominal pain and Jason's colic, and presumably was the causative agent in the abdominal complaints of many Americans similarly infected. The microscopic parasite eluded any visual scope and was resistant to all known antibiotics even if it were detected.The one substance that could cure the infection was found in the Northwest Amazon. Sometimes known simply as the purge, it was most often referred to as ayahuasca.

The plan outlined by Bitu, and hopefully carried out by John, would involve transporting Kelly and Jason soon to Brazil. There in the presence of Rogers, Bitu would administer the ayahuasca to Kelly and Jason, hopefully resulting in a cure. Rogers, who was employed as a consultant for a pharmaceutical research company, would document the experiment and then attempt to reproduce the results back in his lab in a controlled experiment.

Once proven successfully, Bitu would agree to assist Rogers in the cultivation of the plants used in the special tea. In return, a healthy portion of the profits would be fed back to the region through a co-op between Bitu, Rogers and the pharmaceutical company. It was a win-win situation. Rogers was well aware of two key factors. Number one, Bitu was incorporating an as yet unknown plant into his version of ayahuasca. This secret ingredient probably held the key to the drug's effectiveness, and Bitu claimed that he was the only shaman who used it. Secondly, the plants are notoriously fragile outside the rain forest; any attempt to transplant them to another location for cultivation would probably fail. Therefore, Bitu's forest held the trump card--his secret plant would probably not be found anywhere else in the world, ensuring the continued need for preservation. Unfortunately, Rogers passed away before the plan could be instituted.

John's story held a captive audience. Craig and Bob simply sat there, speechless. Either John had gone over the deep end, or they were in the middle of an incredible situation.

" I know this is hard to believe," said John.

" You're not kidding," piped in Craig.

" I suppose it makes sense," said Bob. " But why us?" referring to their obvious involvement.

" We were chosen, I guess," said John.

" Do you mind of I ask you a question?" asked Craig.

" Shoot," said John.

" Can you describe anything specific about Kelly's bedroom?'

John cocked his head and smiled. " You want proof, eh?"

" As a matter of fact, yes," said Craig. " Do you remember anything on her night stand for example?"

John thought for a minute. For Craig, the story was only believable if John's flight to Kelly that night could be verified. Finally John spoke.

" The night stand. Let's see, clock radio, glass of water." So far so good, thought Craig. " And she had a beautiful diamond tennis bracelet right next to the radio."

Craig was stunned. He looked at Bob and nodded. Together they looked at John.   " You son of a bitch!" Craig blurted.

" Where do we go from here?" asked Bob.

John sighed heavily. " We need to convince Kelly that she and her baby need to plan a short vacation, with three strange men, to Brazil."

" How do we do that?" asked Bob.

" I think Craig can persuade her."

" And when am I supposed to see her again?"

" Right now," said John, peering out the window. " Here she comes."

Chapter 20

Kelly's Pain Returns

Craig bolted out of his chair in disbelief. Sure enough, heading up his driveway was Kelly with Jason. He opened the front door before she could knock.

" Hi," he said brightly.

" Hi Craig. I hope I'm not interrupting," she said, glancing over his shoulder at Bob and John. She stared intently at John, who nodded at her.

" No. Not at all. Come in, come in." Craig held the door for her, wondering how his hair looked.

" I wanted to thank you for the other night. I'm afraid I was a bit bothersome, and I'm sorry," she said. Again she stared at John. " Have we met?"

Craig quickly interrupted. " I'm sorry. Kelly Ferguson, this is John Masters and Bob Timmons. We go back to high school and college, respectively." The two nodded.

The next few minutes were filled with tension. The men were suddenly confronted with the key player in their incredible predicament and they weren't prepared for it. They knew at some point they'd need to approach Kelly with their scheme, but the moment didn't feel right.

" Can I get you something to drink?" asked Craig, hoping to lubricate the situation.

" No thank you. Did you tell then about my silly dream?" she asked. Her natural smile put all three at ease. She was a delight to be around, no matter what the situation.

" As a matter of fact, we were just now talking about it," said Craig.

" Oh!" she said, a little embarrassed. Nodding at John, she chuckled and said " Did Craig tell you that I saw you in my room?"

John paused, raised his eyebrows, and spoke softly. " I was there. Kind of a long story."

" I have time," she demanded.

John liked her assertiveness. *Here we go, he thought.* He proceeded to outline the entire story, right down to the trip to Brazil that Bitu had suggested. When he finished, he waited for a response.

" You guys believe this story?" She looked at Craig, who couldn't decide if she was mad or not. " We've barely met and you want me to go to South America with you?"

Immediately, Craig and John realized the ludicrousness of this scheme. How could they have expected Kelly to go along with it? They hardly believed it themselves.

John's mind worked quickly. " This condition of yours, and his, its pretty bad, isn't it?"

She looked at him. She was sure it was him she saw in the room, or rather, in her dream. He was tall, maybe six foot two, thin but muscular, with long straight hair tied in a ponytail. He seemed to be genuinely concerned for her. After all, what did he have to gain from all of this? Finally, she nodded. " My pain hits hard, like my stomach is ready to explode. His must be bad, too. Why else would he cry so hard?"

" Nothing helps?" Craig asked.

" No. I'm willing to try just about anything." She suddenly realized the meaning of that statement. " What is this stuff, exactly?"

John explained, as best he could, the constituents and properties of ayahuasca. He concentrated heavily on its many medicinal uses in the forest. Some tribes, he explained, used it almost exclusively to cure their sick, and had done so for hundreds, perhaps thousands, of years. Regardless of the mysteriousness of soul flight and telepathy, he added, the tea was a proven purgative, resulting in instantaneous cures of poisonings and gastrointestinal problems.

" But you can only use it in the rain forest, right? I mean, it's not something you can get around here?" Kelly asked. Maybe she was more open minded than they thought.

" Well, not exactly," stated John. " I have a network of friends who can ship it to my door, and have done so." He paused, looking first at Craig, then Bob. " In fact, we just had some here a few weeks ago."

Bob then decided to try a new angle. " If we could get some more, would you be willing to try it here?" They all looked at Kelly, waiting for a response.

" Could I take you up on that drink offer?" she evaded the question.

" Coming right up," said Craig as he headed for the kitchen.

" I'd like to read up on this stuff before I make any decisions," she said, surprisingly receptive. She wondered if she should reveal the weird dream she'd had a few nights ago, in which Craig gave her the strange liquid medicine.

" I've got some notes you can read," said Craig as he returned with a glass of lemonade. " I dug up a lot of info at the library. It's really fascinating. You can show it to your husband, see what a doctor thinks."

" No!" she stated emphatically. " I mean, I'd like to keep Kyle out of this at least for right now."

Craig looked at John, who shrugged. They had figured all along that Kelly would be participating with the approval and knowledge of her husband, if at all. Apparently, that was not the case.

" You don't think he'd approve?" John asked.

" Kyle is very proud of his work, but he's very open minded toward alternative medicine." She paused. " The problem is that he doesn't know about my condition."

" Why would you hide it, if you don't mind my asking?"

" He knows about it, but he's under the impression that I'm over it. I just don't want him to worry about me, that's all."

Obviously, it would be a major obstacle to their Brazil trip if Kyle were against it. Regardless of the big picture, John, in no way, wanted to interfere with their marital bliss. As far as he was concerned, without Kelly and Kyle together agreeing about this plan, he'd call it off. Bitu would just have to understand. On the other hand, if Kelly could conceal the whole plan somehow, that would be another story.

Kelly set down the empty lemonade glass. Grabbing the library notes from Craig, she stood with Jason. " I appreciate what you guys are trying to do. I'll have to think about it." Turning to Craig, she smiled, lighting up the room. " Thanks again."

" My pleasure," he said as he held the door for her and watched as she walked home.

" She's really something," said Bob.

" Yeah. This could get really interesting," added John.

Kelly's head was reeling as she entered her house. The whole idea was spectacular, and yet if it worked . . .she began to imagine how nice it would be to enjoy Jason without the constant crying. And her own pains, that was another story. She thought Dr. Moorehead may be on the right track, but what if it turned out to be a dead end? She was about to relax on the sofa and read about ayahuasca when a sharp pain tore through her stomach. Barely able to set Jason down without dropping him, she doubled over on the floor, nearly blacking out. The pain was so intense she was having difficulty breathing. Jason began screaming as well, and Kelly watched in horror as he rolled too far on the sofa and fell helplessly onto the floor, amplifying his cries. Unable to move, she watched in terror as Jason rolled around on the floor, begging for the comforting grasp of his mother's arms. The last thing Kelly saw before she blacked out from the pain was the title of an article that had fallen on the floor next to her: *Ayahuasca, The Great Amazon Cure All.*

Chapter 21

Consenting Adults

Craig was pacing incessantly in his family room, making John nervous.

" They teach you that in law school?" John asked.

" Sorry," said Craig, sitting down.

" Tell me what you're thinking," pleaded John. " Do you still have doubts?"

" Of course I do!" Craig blurted. " This whole thing sounds crazy."

" What if Kelly decides she wants to do it?"

" In that case, I'll go along. But I sure as hell don't want to pressure her."

" Deal. If she comes back to us, we'll initiate the plan. If she balks, we'll never bring it up again."

" Fair enough," said Craig, somewhat relieved. " This stuff could really be the cure, couldn't it?"

" I've seen it used successfully dozens of times. There are already a few pharmaceutical companies in phase I of testing.

Unfortunately, they're all scared of the hallucinogenic properties. They don't seem to realize that the visions are all part of the cure."

" What would happen to Kelly after the experiment?"

" She'd go on with her life, healthier than ever."

" Just like that?" asked Craig, dubiously. " Like the drug researchers wouldn't hound her for follow up research?"

" No. There'd be no need. They're not going to initiate any research until the results can be duplicated in a controlled experiment. Kelly and Jason won't have any further involvement." John paused. " I just hope she's open minded and adventurous enough to be willing to try this."

Kelly woke up after blacking out to the screams of Jason. Sitting up to catch her breath, she picked up her baby and started nursing him. She was terrified. Never had the pain been so bad as to cause her to faint. What if she'd had Jason in the bathtub? He surely could have drowned. Or what about behind the wheel? She didn't even want to think about that. She began to think again about

the ayahuasca experiment. *What have I got to lose, she thought.*

Then again, why should she believe those crazy guys she hardly

knew? *Hardly knew!* Suddenly she was seized with an incredible

realization. How did those guys know about her condition? Picking

her own brain, she could never recall mentioning it to them. She

couldn't believe she hadn't realized it before. *How did they know?*

Setting down her now sleeping baby, she dug in her purse for

the scrap paper that Craig had written his phone number on the night

of her dream. Rolling and unrolling the paper in her hands, she

debated. Oh, what the hell.

" Hello?" Craig answered.

" Hi. It's Kelly."

" Hi. What's up?" Craig gestured to John that it was Kelly.

" We need to talk,"

" Any time."

" Right now?" she asked.

" Sure. Come over."

Craig hung up the phone and looked over to a smiling John. "
On her way."

Within minutes Kelly and Jason were once again sitting in
Craig's family room. She looked at them quizzically. " There's no
immediately apparent explanation as to how you knew about my
stomach problems," she began. " Even Kyle thinks they've stopped.
Obviously, something weird is going on here. I'm still not buying
your story about telepathy and soul flight, but the literature on
ayahuasca speaks for itself."

John nodded. "There's still a lot we don't understand. We just
don't want you to think . . ."

"Don't worry about what I think," she said, surprisingly stern.
"I make my own decisions."

"Of course," said Craig, taken back by her sudden assertiveness.

"Tomorrow I have an appointment with a gastroenterologist.
Kyle will not know a thing about it. Upon receiving a second

opinion on my condition, I will make a decision, and you will be notified."

"Please don't sound angry," John pleaded.

"I'm sorry. I'm just a little nervous about going behind my husband's back. I realize that you guys are really trying to help, but I'm also aware that you need me as well, in order to execute this strange plan of yours. And again, I won't consider traveling to Brazil until after I've tried ayahuasca here first. If that experiment works out, then maybe, I repeat, maybe, I'll go to Brazil with you to visit your shaman friend." She looked up to the ceiling and whispered. "God help me." Looking at John, she asked, "When can you get another supply?"

John was caught off guard. "I'll make a few calls today. It shouldn't take long."

"All right, then." She stood and turned toward Craig, smiling. "Mother told me there'd be days like this."

He nodded. "We're as confused as you are, believe me."

"I'll be in touch," she said, and headed out the door.

Craig stood at the door watching as she traversed the now familiar path to her house. He admired her tenacity. With very few facts, she had made an intelligent decision to attempt an unusual therapy on a condition that had resisted all conventional treatments. Perhaps it was women's intuition that had convinced her that ayahuasca would solve her problems and that these men who were complete strangers a week ago, were sincerely trying to help her. He only hoped that, if nothing else, no harm would befall the charming young woman he'd come to admire so strongly.

"Don't worry," stated John as he emerged from the kitchen with two beers. As if reading Craig's mind, he said, "If something goes wrong and she sues, we've got a top notch lawyer on our side."

"Yeah, right." Craig said as he popped the beer. Gesturing to the phone, he said "all yours."

John looked at his watch. "I guess I could try now."

He watched as Craig left the room to attend to a few chores. His first attempt went through.

"This is Shaman John. I'm ready for my shipment."

"She agreed?" asked the gravely voice at the other end.

"Not yet, but it looks good."

"Four days OK?"

"Perfect."

"Which address?"

"Use the PO out of Lancaster," said John. He used different post office boxes, just in case.

"Keep us posted."

"You bet." John hung up as Craig was entering. "All set. Should be here next week."

"Where you going to do it? Here again?"

"You want to do it again?" John asked.

"Well yeah. I thought that was part of the plan."

"Sure. I just wasn't positive. What about Bob?"

"I think he's up for it. He'd like to try some traveling, actually."

John laughed. "Without a guide, that's probably not such a hot idea." Finishing his beer, John stood to leave. "I'm sure Kelly will call you as soon as she finds out what this other doctor has to say."

"Yeah, I'll let you know."

"All right. Later," John said as he left.

Agent Dressens watched John through binoculars from his unmarked van, parked inconspicuously up the street. Listening in on John's phone conversation, he was encouraged by the news that John was expecting a shipment soon. Unfortunately, the mailing address was too vague, so his day to day surveillance would have to continue. He wanted to be in striking distance when John went to pick up his special package. He would stop at nothing to get his hands on John's tea.

Chapter 22

Second Opinion

"What am I doing?" Kelly said audibly as she pulled into the parking lot of Dr. Emory Thompson's office. After going to the trouble of leaving Jason with her mother and driving across town, she realized the futility of the appointment. If she really needed conventional treatment, her husband could've handled it just as well. She almost felt as if she were cheating on Kyle by seeing another doctor.

But more importantly, she was becoming increasingly convinced that she had to try ayahuasca regardless of the results of this examination. So often in life people are guided by convictions that have no rational basis. The ayahuasca incident was such an event for Kelly. Despite the lack of any concrete, scientific evidence in favor of taking the tea, she nonetheless believed it would work.

Reluctantly, she entered the doctor's office. It took fifteen minutes to fill out the new patient form. She'd decided not to mention the fact that she was Kyle's wife, just in case Dr. Thompson knew Kyle.

"Please have a seat. The doctor will be with you shortly," smiled the receptionist as she took the clipboard with Kelly's information. Kelly sat down and began searching for a magazine. She wondered how long Kyle's patients usually had to wait.

Finally, she was escorted into Dr. Thompson's examination room. The black exam table was frayed from years of usage, and the diplomas on the wall were separated from the rest of the world by a thick layer of dust. The sphygmomanometer looked as if it could be donated to a museum and the bare light bulb over a small desk completely eroded her confidence. She probably would have snuck out and escaped if it wasn't for the sudden arrival of Dr. Thompson's ancient nurse.

"Here. You'll have to put this on," she snapped as she handed Kelly a faded paper gown.

"Is this really necessary?" asked Kelly.

"Yes. Please remove all clothing and jewelry."

Kelly was shocked. She wouldn't imagine what type of examination would require such a measure. Even during her last gynecological exam she didn't have to remove all clothing. Dutifully obeying, however, she changed into the robe and waited for what seemed like a long time considering she saw no other patients in the office. Finally, after knocking once, Dr. Thompson entered.

He was one of those physicians whose poor physical appearance contrasted his role as healer. He was a stooped man whose most noticeable feature was a crop full of gray hair sprouting vociferously from each ear. Kelly nearly recoiled in disgust. She accepted that all doctors eventually grow old, but this seemed unbelievable.

"Good morning, Mrs. . . .um..Ferguson," he said, reading her chart without looking up. "Got some stomach problems, eh?"

"Yes. It's a sharp pain that comes and goes," she said, giving him the benefit of the doubt. He immediately pulled up a stool, and looking up to view the low end of his bifocals, began palpating her abdomen. His fingernails appeared infested with a raging fungal infection.

"Does this hurt?" he asked, pressing hard.

"No."

"Here?"

"No."

"How about here?"

"No."

"Triggered by anything? Food? Exercise?"

"No. No pattern, really." She was not being a good patient.

"Hmm." Pushing away from her, he continued. "I'd like to do an endoscopy. It involves . . ."

"I'm familiar with the procedure," Kelly interrupted. She decided to pick his brain. "Do you suspect H.Pylori?" She'd remembered Kyle's enthusiasm about curing one of his patients with an antibiotic regimen.

"Possible. We could test for that too." Kelly didn't know there was a test for it. "It usually requires trial and error."

"Are there other infections or parasites that might be responsible?"

"Not easy to detect, if so. Like what, worms or something?"

"I don't know. Just thinking out loud."

Thompson shook his head, then coughed. "Here," tearing off a slip from his pad. "Take this to Miss Hawkins, and she'll set up an appointment. Stick to bland foods, and no aspirin."

He left abruptly, and Kelly figured she'd never see him again. Offering no new information and reinforcing her conviction that conventional therapy was useless, she dressed and headed for the receptionist.

"Shall we bill your insurance?" asked Hawkins.

"Yes. Please. And I'll call later to set up my appointment for the endoscopy." She lied.

Kelly left, angry that she'd wasted her time but now anxious to experiment herself. Somehow, she trusted her new friends, and the ayahuasca had almost become an obsession with her. Partly as a

result of her wanting to be rid of her affliction and partly because of

her desire to take control of her own life, Kelly saw the tea as a

fantastic opportunity. She now had to deal with the details and the

nagging decision whether to keep it from Kyle. In the end she

decided that what he didn't know wouldn't hurt him, but that only

made the logistics more difficult. It would involve a night alone,

with three virtual strangers. She was suddenly depressed at the

realization that such an arrangement would be nearly impossible.

She drove on, contemplating her dilemma of how to get away for a

night. Just one night, to change her whole life around.

Chapter 23

Surprise Conference

Kyle stared blankly into his beer. The cocktail lounge of the hotel was nearly empty, which suited him fine, as he was in no mood for meaningless banter. With all that had been going on at the hospital he'd nearly forgotten about the conference. He had been worried that Kelly would protest, but she was strangely supportive. He knew the time away might be good for him, but he was surprised that she felt the same way. Deciding not to over analyze the situation, he downed his beer and ordered another.

The Eighth Annual Conference on Internal Medicine was taking place in Hilton Head, South Carolina. Feeling not at all sociable, Kyle planned to bury himself in the conferences, and when time permitted, the hotel lounge. The whirlwind conference began early Saturday morning and ran through Sunday evening. Kyle was expecting to get home late that night. It was the first time he'd left for a weekend since having Jason around, and it felt weird. He concluded that he'd never be able to handle a job that required a lot of traveling. He also realized how much he missed Kelly. In response, he'd decided a few drinks might help him sleep. He wondered how Kelly was doing as he downed his third beer.

* * *

Kelly was beside herself with excitement. Like Kyle, she had completely forgotten about his conference. Normally, she would have dreaded his leaving for a weekend. This time, however, the turn of events played right into her hands. She was rocking Jason asleep in her arms, preparing to make two phone calls. The first would be to her mother and would involve an outright lie. It was obvious to Kelly that her mom wouldn't understand the ayahuasca therapy, so she concocted a story about going to visit a friend until late Saturday night, and wondered if grandma would like to baby-sit. Kelly would pump her breast milk to keep Jason satisfied, and would pick him up on Sunday. If that plan worked, Kelly would call Craig to set up the session. As Jason fell asleep, Kelly dialed her mother a bit nervously.

"Hello?" Adelle Babcox was widowed over ten years ago, and clung to her relationship with Kelly and Kelly's younger sister, Debby. She was used to life alone, but was always happy to baby-sit Jason.

"Hi mom."

"Hi dear, how are you?"

"OK, I guess. Kyle's in Hilton Head for that stupid conference."

"Honey, it's probably not stupid to Kyle."

"I know. I'm just kidding. Would you like to do me a favor?"

"Sure, what's up?"

"I was thinking about visiting my friend, Melissa. Remember her?"

"Oh yeah. The one that lives in Cleveland?"

"That's her. Do you think you could watch Jason overnight?"

Adelle had made no secret of the fact that she'd love to watch Jason overnight some time. As a grandmother, she believed that she had the magic touch that could put Jason to sleep at night. Now was her chance. "I'd love to!"

"Great! I'll pump tonight so you'll have plenty of milk."

"What time?"

"How about four or five?"

"Perfect. I'll see you then."

Kelly hung up; thinking that was too easy. With that out of the way, and feeling only slightly guilty, she searched for Craig's number. Taking a deep breath, she dialed.

"Hello?"

"Craig?"

"Speaking."

So businesslike, she thought. "This is Kelly."

"Oh! What's up?"

"I believe our window of opportunity has arrived," she said, feeling as if she were involved in an affair.

"What's that?" Craig wasn't quick to catch on.

"Kyle's out of town this weekend, and I got a baby-sitter for tomorrow night. I think that would be a good opportunity for our little experiment."

"Wow! That's great. Let me call John and I'll call you right back."

"Craig, wait."

"Yeah?"

"Are you sure this is a good idea? I mean, what if something goes wrong?"

"I can't imagine what. You'll be in good hands."

"OK. I'm just a little nervous, that's all. I'll wait for your call."

"OK."

As she hung up, Kelly could feel her stomach rumble, although not with the usual intensity. She decided that she'd be happy either way. Just as well if tomorrow was bad for everyone, but she was excited at the prospect of curing her stomach. She pulled a Coke out of the fridge and waited for the phone call.

John had fallen asleep on the couch watching television when the phone rang.

"Master's residence."

"John?"

"Hi Craig. What's going on?"

"You sound like you were crashed."

"I was. What's up?"

"Kelly called. She wondered if tomorrow night would be cool."

"Hell yes! My shipment arrived yesterday. When tomorrow?"

"She didn't say. I told her I'd call her back."

"Can we make it around seven, your place?"

"Fine by me," Craig said.

"I'll come over early and we'll go over our game plan. Just be prepared, make her comfortable with the whole thing."

"Good idea. I'll call her right now and set it up."

As Kelly prepared herself and Jason for bed, she tried to keep her mind off the experiment. Thinking about it too much would only interfere with a good night's sleep, not that she'd be able to sleep after the nightmare incident anyway. Instead, her thoughts shifted to Kyle, hoping his conference was going well. If only he knew what she had planned for the next evening. She chuckled aloud at the realization that tomorrow night at this time she'd be consuming an exotic hallucinogenic medicine with three men she barely knew while her husband was out of town. What could possibly go wrong?

Chapter 24

Bail Out

John let himself in upon arriving at Craig's house Saturday morning, as the door was unlocked and there was no answer. Immediately he heard the drone of the vacuum cleaner, mixing cacophonously with the stereo. Craig finally noticed John, who had worked his way to the dining room, and shut off the vacuum.

John shook his head as he gently removed his backpack. "This isn't exactly a dinner party."

"It needed it, believe me," said Craig, gesturing to the vacuum. Craig didn't consider himself to be a fastidious housekeeper, but his bachelor friends liked to rub him about his cleaning habits. Because of Ritchie's cat hair alone, Craig needed to vacuum at least every other day.

"Come on. I'll finish later." Craig led John to the family room.

"Bob said he'd be here around four," said John as he unpacked his backpack. Aside from a jar of ayahuasca similar to the last one, there were numerous other vials containing unidentified powders and elixirs. "I'll explain later."

"Is this the same stuff we had before?"

"Yeah, with a few additions to intensify the effect. I'm not sure we'll use them though."

"I hope Kelly handles this OK."

"I wanted to talk to you about that."

"What do you mean?"

"I think it would be wise if either you or Bob stayed clean tonight. Designated baby-sitter if you know what I mean."

"I volunteer," Bob said as he entered the family room.

"You sure?" asked Craig. "I'd be happy to."

"No, that's OK, really. I'd kind of like to observe, anyway."

"OK then, that's settled," said John. "What time is Kelly coming over?"

"She said about seven," replied Craig.

"That gives us a few hours," said John, glancing at his watch. "As long as we don't have any interruptions we'll be OK."

Dressens smiled as he observed the arrivals of John Masters and Bob Timmons at Craig's house. He knew something was up, and was banking on the assumption that he would catch Masters red handed with his ayahuasca. Finally. He would wait for nightfall, visually inspect the house, then make his move.

He figured there was no need for a backup, as he had the element of surprise on his side. He doubted there would be any resistance. With efficiency of movement, he eased himself to the back of the van and began donning his black clothing.

Kelly glanced hesitantly in the mirror. She knew she had no reason to care about her appearance but primped anyway. Based on Craig's advice to dress comfortably, she chose her running suit. It was not very flattering, but very practical. Finally, she decided it was time to go. Already she felt her stomach grumble. Craig had also advised that she skip dinner. Nervously checking the kitchen and family room for something, anything that she forgot to do, she finally grabbed her keys and opened the front door. *You're not going on vacation, she told herself, just a night out.* Locking the

door, she made her way toward Craig's.

It was an unseasonably cool night, a reminder of summer's

transient quality. All was quiet and normal, except the cars in

Craig's driveway. There was also a plain white van across the street.

She hoped that there would be no surprise guests. Mustering all her

courage, she crossed the street and approached Craig's driveway.

Here goes nothing.

Craig was waiting at the door as she arrived.

"Hi. Come on in," he said, holding the door. Kelly noticed

Craig's curious gaze at the white van. Stepping in, she nodded to

Bob and John.

John stood to greet her. "Are we ready?"

"Ready as I'll ever be."

"Good. Do you have any questions?"

"How did I ever agree to this?" she laughed.

John smiled, and with a fraternal pat on her back ushered her into the kitchen. "Here's the main attraction," he said, gesturing to the ayahuasca.

Kelly stared at the kitchen table, not knowing what to say. Aside from a jar full of a cloudy brown liquid, there were two vials of white powders and a dropper bottle with an unknown liquid. The room had an unusual, earthy odor, like what she'd expect from a huge excavation site. She strolled over to the table and picked up a bottle of the powder, examining it closely.

"If this is coke, I'm out of here," she said.

"Not to worry. It's a desiccated powder version of the tea. We probably won't even need it."

"And this?" she asked, holding up the dropper bottle.

"We call it moon shot. It's a tincture made of hallucinogenic jungle seeds."

"I think I'll pass."

"I would too," Bob piped in as he entered the kitchen. Although she had not yet gotten to know Bob, Kelly felt very much at ease around him. His easygoing manner reminded her of her cousin, with whom she was very close.

"Bob will be our designated observer tonight," said John. "Not that we're anticipating any problems, but just in case."

"Good idea," said Kelly. She felt more comfortable already. Carefully, she touched the ayahuasca. "May I?"

"Go ahead."

Kelly picked up the jar. It was full of a dirty brown liquid, devoid of any noticeable particulate matter. Somehow the jar seemed an inappropriate container for such an exotic substance. Holding it up to the light, she noticed that she could barely see through it. "So this is it?"

"That's it," said John. "Three doses."

Suddenly Kelly made a very convincing jerk, simulating an accidental drop. She saw John's eyes practically pop out of his head.

"Just kidding," she said, setting it on the table carefully. "This stuff means a lot to you, doesn't it?"

John smiled as he looked at Craig, shaking his head. "I think we're in for a great night."

Bob was staring intently out the window.

"What is it?" asked Craig.

"I don't know. Thought I saw something."

"Probably Ritchie. He's out."

"Probably."

Dressens was motionless against the wall of Craig's house. He'd seen all he needed to see. However, the presence of the girl disturbed him. He felt comfortable storming the house and covering the original three suspects. The additional person made him uneasy. It would be much more difficult to handle the arrest alone. He did not anticipate any violence, but couldn't rule it out. Regardless, he knew there was no backing down. He had his man.

His original plan was to enter through the back. However, as he examined the house, he decided it would be easier to corner his suspects in the front room. Quietly, he double-checked his holster, readying himself for the arrest. Suddenly, he heard the door open and slipped behind a nearby tree.

Bob had decided to execute a quick inspection of the yard. He knew he saw something, and wanted to rule out any intruders. Walking around the front yard, he noticed the van. There was something unusual about the van but he couldn't figure it out. Satisfied that nothing was amiss, he reentered the front door.

John, Craig and Kelly were already getting settled in the family room. John was explaining more about the tea to Kelly, who was a captive audience. He was explaining its long and mythical history, as well as its impressive list of therapeutic uses. Finally, he described the effects so Kelly could be somewhat prepared.

"If it's such an effective purge, should I be prepared to make a run for the can?" she asked.

"I doubt you'll have to rush. It probably won't have that dramatic of an effect."

"Well? What are we waiting for?" she asked, sitting up in her chair. Craig was encouraged by her enthusiasm.

Suddenly, Bob rushed to the front window. The van . . . the plain hub caps . . . The Federal license plates . . . "Get your shit, all of it!" he said, grabbing John. "Get the hell out of here."

Craig was obviously shocked. "What the fuck are you doing?"

"Stay here," Bob commanded. He grabbed Kelly's hand. John had already thrown everything into his backpack. Craig was watching with astonishment as the three slipped out to the back and into the night. Simultaneously, his front door exploded open, and he stared at blue steel.

"Freeze!" Commanded Dressens.

"Shit! What's this all about?" Craig cried.

"Where's your friends?" demanded Dressens. Already, he sensed his mission was doomed.

"What are you talking about?" Craig caught on quickly, impressed by Bob's split second thinking, but not at all happy with the confrontation.

His gun pointed at Craig, Dressens moved laterally to peer into the now empty kitchen. He looked back at Craig, whose arms were shooting straight up. Masters, and his tea, were gone. He knew he had nothing on Craig. Slamming his gun into his holster, he kicked open the front screen door and stormed out cursing. Craig inched up to the door and watched as Dressens peeled out in his van.

Frightened and confused, he went to the kitchen, doubtful but hoping that his friends were hiding in his back yard. Silently, he eased out to the deck. Looking out to the blackness, he could see nothing. Suddenly, something pushed his leg. Jumping with fright, he turned to face his attacker. He sighed with relief. It was Ritchie, purring loudly. He'd missed his dinner.

Chapter 25

Colonel Gibbons

"Let me get this straight." Colonel Gibbons was not a man to beat around the bush. As the CIA commander whose responsibilities involved the mind enhancement research at Wood Labs, he was not interested in guesswork. He began to pace in front of his desk. "So far, your research has concluded that by giving hallucinogens to monkeys we can increase their mental capacities. OK. So you want me to suggest to the President that he drink this hallucinogenic tea from the Amazon, and, aside from a few major hallucinogenic episodes, he'll be able to think more clearly?" He slammed his fist on his desk. "You call yourselves fucking researchers? Are you sure it's the monkeys drinking that shit?"

Roger Temple stroked his beard nervously. Like most scientists, he hated pressure, and sitting in Gibbon's office with no concrete data to present was about as much pressure as he could imagine. "There's more to it than that. Obviously, we're not suggesting that we subject the President to a drug trip. We're in the process of isolating the cortical enhancing chemicals from the psychotropic ones. We hope to boost mental capabilities without the hallucinogenic side effects." If nothing else, Temple believed he was on the right track. "The monkey results were encouraging."

"Yeah, that's where you cut monkey brains into lunch meat slices after getting them stoned and counting their nerve endings?" Gibbons was beyond sarcastic. He did not like to be toyed with. "What controls did you use?"

"Other non-drugged brain tissue." Temple knew that was a weak link to the research. So far he could not design an experiment that compared the same monkey brain before and after the ayahuasca. Using two different monkeys wouldn't convince anybody in a peer review.

"Another monkey entirely. As anyone observing this conversation could see, there is great variation between brain tissue of two members of the same species." Gibbons stared disgustedly at Temple. Sitting down at his desk, he folded his hands in front of him and changed his tone. "Look. The summit in Geneva is four and a half months away. In his present condition, we can't even give the President half the advisory information he needs. Admittedly, you're the only researcher with any chance of helping us."

Temple allowed his anger to quell. His interest in hallucinogens dated all the way back to his dissertation. Unfortunately, the anti drug movement practically killed all research money on the subject. The CIA/Wood grant was paltry compared to private sector research money, and because the project was classified he had no hope of publishing his study. But he was researching hallucinogens and the grant money kept him and his family fed with a roof over their heads, so he put up with bureaucratic headaches. He also had gained a lot of respect for Gibbons after learning about his resume. Gibbons was an organic chemist working on synthetic motor oil formulas when he found himself in Kuwait during the oil shortages of the seventies. His research team was detained for months during the embargo, and one day he courageously masterminded their escape to Saudi Arabia. His survivalist attitude, scientific mind and leadership abilities were not unnoticed and the CIA recruited him for their causes. Fair but tough, he was a brute with raw intelligence, and Temple admired him.

" With the samples we've had to work with, we've isolated eight different alkaloids, four of which remain unidentified," Temple continued matter of factly.

" Indoles?" Gibbons asked.

" There were three beta carbolines, all indoles, as well as dimethyltriptamine," answered Temple.

" DMT?"

" Yeah, but not all the samples had it," said Temple. DMT, also known as the businessman's high because it could be used at lunchtime, produced an intense, LSD like trip that lasted only a matter of minutes when smoked. DMT research proved fascinating because most neuroscientists believed that it was a simple enough chemical to possibly exist naturally in the human brain. There was something tantalizing about the notion of humans producing their own natural hallucinogens. " We believe the neuronal regeneration comes from one or more of the unidentified alkaloids."

" Are you sure we're not barking up the wrong tree?" countered Gibbons. "I mean, are we putting any stock in that telepathy crap?"

Remembering that the Wood research was a direct spin-off of the original studies conducted to investigate Rios' predicted assassination, Temple stood and began pacing himself. " We dug into that story. Apparently, telepathic phenomena occur regularly with ayahuasca. Much like the collective soul concept."

" Along the lines of Jung?" asked Gibbons, referring to the famed psychologist.

" Similar. But ayahuasca encompasses all of existence, animals and plants as well as the spiritual world," said Temple. He could see Gibbon's expression turn sour. " Just filling you in on the folklore."

" What about human experimentation?" asked Gibbons.

Temple was surprised by Gibbon's straightforward approach. "We're looking for volunteers. I'm designing the cognition tests already. We've got several isolates in capsule form that we can compare in a double blind."

" What about the unknowns?" Gibbons pressed on.

" Within a week we'll have those separated out and in capsule form as well. Our plan is to isolate and identify only those that show promise. It will save valuable time." Temple suddenly felt more in

control.

" Safety measures?"

" Full medical and resuscitative staff on duty. We're not that

worried. The toxicological studies were amazing. The LD-50 is

apparently non-existent with the samples we had," said Temple.

LD-50, or lethal dose 50, is a figure used by pharmacologists to

determine the dose of a drug that causes death in fifty percent of the

test subjects. A high or non-existent LD-50 indicates a drug that is

very safe to ingest.   " Unfortunately, we have other problems."

Gibbons gestured for Temple to continue.

" Our test samples will more than likely be used before we can

synthesize our own. We need more." Temple looked across the

room at Dressens.

" Pete?" Gibbons redirected his interview.

Dressens was in charge of collecting ayahuasca samples. It was

turning into an operational nightmare. Plenty of Brazilians were

supplying the tea to the field operatives, but most were phony brews.

The legitimate tea was only found deeper in the forest, and those natives were very suspicious of white men. The few field agents who did get samples discovered that some ayahuasca had a short shelf life, a month or so, before spoiling. Allowing one or two weeks to arrive in Temple's lab gave the researchers a very short period with which to perform their experiments. And that wasn't the only problem. " We've lost three agents so far. Without a trace. They're primitive but cunning," explained Dressens.

"You mean they don't like handing over their sacred tea to a CIA agent armed to the tits and dressed in a three piece suit?" Gibbons' sarcasm returned.

" Many of the shamans don't share their formulas with anybody, let alone whitey," said Dressens. " But there is one exception." He paused.

Again, Gibbons gestured to continue, obviously irritated by the pause.

Dressens took the cue and proceeded. " A guy named Masters. John Masters. Journeyman construction worker from Ohio.

Somehow, he got in good with an elder shaman near the Orinoco River. The samples we got from him were very active," said Dressens.

" How did you track it to him?" asked Gibbons.

" An agent heard about this guy who saved a chieftain's son's life. Since then he kept coming out of the jungle with a lot of supplies."

" What about Customs?"

" Not a problem. All legal. Ayahuasca's status is unclear, and dogs don't sniff it out, anyway. We traced him and stole a small sample."

Gibbons stood. " Dr. Temple says he needs more ayahuasca. Get a warrant and bring this Masters character in."

" Already got one."

" Then what are you waiting for?"

" Nothing."

" One more thing." He turned to Temple. " I want to be there for the human tests."

Chapter 26

El Presidente

Ambassador Manuel Cordova could barely contain himself. In his three years of statesmanship he had hosted countless state dinners for leaders the world over, but never the President of the United States. Vice Presidents, yes. But the leader of the most powerful nation in the world? This would be a night to remember. Perhaps owing to their close proximity, presidential visits to the pan American country were frequent but brief. When the President finally accepted the dinner invitation, it sent the Mexican leadership into an unusual frenzy.

It was no secret that the Mexican Government was more than willing to lay out the red carpet for the American leader. Years of political upheaval, natural disasters and environmental plundering had left the Mexican country in an economic shambles. Most of the country's social programs needed foreign aid for survival and the United States was one of the countries willing to invest capital. Unfortunately, and predictably, it was never enough, and with the exception of several coastal tourist attractions the Mexican infrastructure was crumbling. The Mexicans needed more help, and looked to their northern neighbor with outstretched hands.

For Ronald Reagan, an outstretched hand was there to be shaken. Although aware of the Mexican plight, the details would be left to his advisors and Secretary of State. His visit, much to the disappointment of his hosts, was purely ornamental. He had grown increasingly skilled at delegating responsibility. Ironically, many analysts saw it as political genius. After all, the leadership of the most powerful country in the world should not be left solely to one person. Reagan's reliance on his cabinet was therefore seen by many as shrewd politics. He had his critics, though. To many, Reagan was just plain lazy. His chief of staff, behind the scenes, was always on his toes bolstering the President's image. Ultimately, the President's right hand man had assumed responsibility for a difficult assignment--avoiding public embarrassment of a President gradually losing touch with reality and damage control when those embarrassing incidents did occur.

Pete Mitchell was nervous. None of the rigid Secret Service training and experience he received could prepare him for nights like this. U.S. Presidents traveling abroad are always vulnerable, but Reagan's ambiguous stand on many controversial economic issues surrounding the Mexican economy, combined with that country's unstable political status created a volatile atmosphere. As the President's chief security officer, he had assigned an extra dozen agents to this event, including four Mexican nationals to work undercover in the kitchen. Satisfied that the perimeter of the building was secure and triple checked, that door guards were in place, he stepped up to the dais, where the President would be eating. One final check before dinner.

The Imperial State Building was Mexico's prize jewel of architecture, not counting the Mayan ruins. Used exclusively for state dinners, it was over one hundred years old but remodeled several times since. Crystal chandeliers dotted the ceiling fifty feet up and one hundred cloth-covered tables awaited the full house. The dais table was on a stage five feet high and sixty feet long. The President and First Lady would be among a dozen dignitaries breaking bread, smiling banally and applauding where appropriate. Mitchell would not feel like eating until the President was safely back on Air Force One.

" Ah Mr. Mitchell, I hoped to find you here," said an ebullient

Carlos Pena, Mitchell's counterpart in the Mexican security

contingency.

" Mr. Pena. Yes, everything appears to be in order." Mitchell

didn't share Pena's attitude that there was little threat of an incident

during the dinner. Perhaps it was American arrogance or simply

distrust, but Mitchell felt uneasy about the President's vulnerability.

" I assure you that we will cooperate in any manner that you see

fit."

" Thank you, much obliged." Mitchell's eyes were methodically

scanning the dining area behind his standard issue dark glasses. It

was no accident that Secret Servicemen wore dark glasses.

Avoiding eye contact was paramount for their function as

surveillance experts. It served to make Pena more than a little

uneasy. Nonetheless, he was willing to kiss Mitchell's ass. As a

Mexican Government official, he had no choice.

The guests began arriving around five o'clock with dinner scheduled for seven. One by one, Mexico's elite citizens filed into the Imperial Building and found their assigned seats. The pretty people of Mexico were excited about the party of the century.

Amid thunderous applause, the dignitaries began their entrance and the slow progression down the red carpet runway to the head table. Mitchell stood with the President and First Lady waiting their turn. Hearing the signal, he nodded to the two head agents and the procession began. Mitchell thought Reagan looked a bit tired, but ignored it. He wished he hadn't

As the final dignitaries were seated at the dais, Mitchell took his place at the corner of the stage, taking quick glances at the crowd and verifying the presence of his agents. Returning his gaze to the President, he heard a scream and saw from the corner of his eye the nightmarish vision every Secret Serviceman dreads. The President, apparently unconscious, lay slumped at the table, his face on his dinner plate.

Mitchell charged to the President while his agents flanked the stage, guns drawn. As he covered the distance in double time, he approached the President. There was no sign of blood or foul play whatsoever, although the First Lady had by now ducked under his arm for support.

" Mr. President?" yelled Mitchell.

Amidst the confusion, Mitchell thought he heard someone snoring. There was silence, followed by--yes, it was snoring!

The Mexican Ambassador sitting next to Reagan began to smile, then laugh audibly.

"El Presidente is napping!" he bellowed.

Soon the entire dais was laughing. Mitchell was embarrassed, but not for himself personally. If this is bad, he thought, wait for the morning newspapers.

Chapter 27

Temple's Secret

"Dr. Temple to see you," the intercom buzzed in Malcolm Swenson's office. Swenson was the Chief Executive Officer of Wood Pharmaceuticals. He was perusing the Wall Street Journal and surprised by the early hour of Temple's visit.

"Send him in." He stood to greet the research scientist. Putting out his hand he shook Temple's with the firm grip of a man used to being in charge. "Roger, how are you?"

Temple smiled at Swenson. He was a corpulent man, six foot four and two hundred sixty pounds. His career started in medicinal chemistry, just as Temple's, but had taken an administrative turn two decades ago. Swenson was just as out of place in a modern chemistry lab as Temple would be in a board meeting. Yet, their common background gave them a bond, and as the senior research scientist on one of Wood's most lucrative contracts, Temple was treated with warmth and respect in Swenson's office.

Temple had a great deal of respect for Swenson as well. In the real, hard world of big business, it took visionary leadership to succeed in multinational commerce. The Pharmaceutical Industry was an extremely competitive arena to test one's business skills, and Swenson proved to be a capable executive. Anticipating the generic drug industry boon, he created a separate division within Wood, called Genwood, to manufacture a full line of generic drugs. Wood was also one of the first major drug companies to pull out of vaccine research and development, in part due to the liability issues generated by the swine flu fiasco of 1976. Twice fighting off hostile merger attempts, Wood turned the tide and itself acquired two smaller, very successful laboratories. Wood was growing, and its stockholders were smiling. The Special Biologics Division was another notch on the bedpost. Swenson was confident that Temple would succeed in developing a marketable drug in the promising field of Alzheimer's research, and had bimonthly meetings with him to stay current.

"How did the meeting with Gibbons go?" asked Swenson.

"He's a tough man," sighed Temple. "He knows we're doing the best we can but he's getting impatient."

"Who can blame him?" Swenson said, pointing to the front-page photo of Reagan asleep at the state dinner in Mexico.

Temple shook his head. "I heard about that. I remember falling asleep at a dinner party once. You never live it down."

Swenson bellowed a laugh. "No sir. Especially if you happen to be the President of the United States." His smile quickly faded as he stood. "Why don't you fill me in?"

"On the research?"

"Well frankly, I don't give a shit about your bowling scores."

"I don't bowl," Temple said innocently, then realized his folly. "Sorry. Anyway, there's good news and bad news. The good news is that we've isolated eight distinct compounds from the most active sample. The bad news is that three remain a complete mystery. The problem is that we need to discover which combination is responsible for the neural effects and which ration is required of each constituent."

"So it's possible that the three unknowns are inactive anyway."

"Possible. We'll test later this week on the five known isolates with as many ratios as we can manage. If we get results we may assume that the three unknowns aren't necessary to the blend. The key factor is time. We need to reach a conclusion either way by the end of the month or Gibbons may pull the plug."

Swenson was pacing calmly behind his desk. His normally decisive brain was having trouble. He couldn't decide if the good news outweighed the bad. "I'd like to see your research notes."

The request, or demand, caught Temple off guard. Generally speaking, most researchers keep copious records of experimental results. The notes are closely guarded secrets. From a legal standpoint, no matter who the researcher contracts with, the notes are a personal possession, like a diary. The accepted mentality is that if the research is fruitful, the end product is all that counts and is patent protected. On the other hand, if the end product is a failure then the research notes are worthless as well. The bottom line is that researchers usually keep possession of their notes, except for the required paperwork that the sponsor requests. In many cases, the notes are practically illegible to anyone else. At any rate, Temple was surprised by Swenson's demand.

"Sure. May I ask why?"

"Please don't be defensive," Swenson smiled at him. "I'm not going to steal anything. I'm just curious. You must admit, this is one of the most interesting projects we've seen in a while."

Temple had to agree. Besides, what harm would it cause? "I hope you can read some of it."

"No problem. I'll just look at the pictures."

Somehow Swenson's smile was not comforting to Temple. He almost could sense that something was up, but couldn't put a finger on it.

"I'll bring it by tonight."

"Good. Is there anything we can do for you?

"Well, we're still waiting for more samples, but I know that's not your department."

"Unfortunately not. I can't help but think that we'd be a little more efficient in tracking down the shaman's brew. How critical is it?"

"Not as bad as I originally thought. We made some breakthroughs that really bought us time. It's all in my notes." Temple realized after he said it that Swenson might take it the wrong way. Fortunately, Swenson changed the subject.

"Hopefully, we'll beat the budget cuts." He was referring to the budget slashing proposal, which would cut millions out of the FDA budget and result in huge delays in the drug approval process.

"I get the impression they'd push this one through anyway."

"You're probably right. Well, thanks for stopping by," Swenson said abruptly. "I'll look forward to looking at the research notes."

"You got it." Temple spoke as he rose and shook Swenson's hand.

As he exited the ornate office, Temple breathed a sigh of relief. He was glad that the only request to come out of the meeting was to see his research notes. After all, Temple was clever enough not to

mention in his notes why he had used so much of the ayahuasca.

Chapter 28

Politics As Usual

Bitu watched the black smoke settle into the valley of souls. On still days with no wind to disturb the atmosphere, the exhaust fumes from earth moving machines would waft into the valley and settle malignantly over the forest canopy. Bitu had never seen the machines but knew of them. Their smoke was thicker and darker than wood fires, and those who ventured into the valley reported the awful smell it imparted to their otherwise virgin nares.

One does not need a university degree to attain wisdom. Bitu's wisdom was the result of lifelong lessons from living the way of nature and his association with ayahuasca. The lessons he learned over the past few years were distressing. Although he and his tribe had resisted acculturation up to now, he knew the lure of modern society would be too much for the younger members to resist. Instinctively, he knew the only hope would be to thwart the encroachment of the new society onto his sacred grounds. Countless sessions with the tea yielded no answers. Then one night, after a solo session, the vine spoke to him and delivered a powerful message.

At first, Bitu was reluctant to accept the message. He knew nothing about strange stomach afflictions and white man's need for new medicines from the rain forest. However, the repeated message grew stronger in each successive session and soon he decided to act on them. By that time, he had grown trust John Masters, despite his decision to withhold his most cherished secrets. John was a dedicated apprentice and had earned a great deal of respect within the tribe. However, he was a white man and therefore could not rightfully gain the knowledge passed down through the ages.

As stories of the encroachment became more frequent, Bitu knew his time was running out. A messenger told him that thirty suns ago the yellow monsters had destroyed the village of Beligo, where Bitu's cousins lived. Bitu decided that his final days would be dedicated to the preservation of his people's way of life, no matter what the method. Pushing into his seventh decade, Bitu would nevertheless become the nemesis of a host of intruders from the New World. Their claims over his lands would be met with the wrath of a genuine warrior.

Many scientists seriously believe that the continued destruction of the rain forest of the tropics will have deleterious effects on the remainder of the planet. Indeed, it has been generally recognized by ecologists that major environmental disasters in one part of the world almost certainly impact others. Obvious examples abound, such as the dust clouds from volcanoes and tidal waves from sub oceanic earthquakes. Less obvious, but equally dramatic examples are the draining of the wetlands and the proliferation of the   " concrete jungle". In the case of the rain forests, the impact involves climatologic, biologic and sociologic concerns. The question is not whether something should be done, but rather if it is too late for something to be done.

Fortunately, there are enough optimists around who believe it is not too late. These optimists fall into two camps. The first camp comprises those who subscribe to Lovelock's 1972 Gaia hypothesis which concluded that the planet earth behaves like a single living entity and is extremely adaptable to environmental challenges. In fact, it was Lovelock who discovered the ozone hole over Antarctica but denounced its importance because the earth, or Gaia, could adapt. Similarly, any destruction of the rain forest would be counterbalanced by climactic or biologic adaptations, keeping the earth's overall ecology in a balanced state. The Gaia hypothesis retains and inspires many followers to this day.

The second camp of optimists is a little less romantic. They are sometimes referred to as capitalists, and they believe that money can solve most of the world's problems. In the case of the rain forest they are probably right. As of 1993, no less than twelve major research teams were working in the rain forest in search of medicinal plants. The implications were simple. A promising drug entity that could be patented and marketed would provide the capital to preserve the very forest that produced it. Why bulldoze when cultivation and preservation is more profitable?

The CIA seems an unlikely player in the arena, but in fact their motives were more numerous and more profit based than anybody's. The political reasons were almost too complex for anyone to understand, but the interest in medicinal plants was not difficult to appreciate. As the American economy began to crumble under the weight of health care costs, it became imperative to search for promising new drugs to sustain and improve life. For the CIA it was a simple matter of discovering the magic bullets before another country did. Gaining the edge, as always, their prime directive. And especially in the case of mind enhancement chemicals. The race was on.

Colonel Gibbons knew the stakes were high and the risks great. The shamans were far from cordial, their turf hostile. Any research team that entered the rain forest would certainly encounter several unknowns. Although the South American continent was almost completely explored, there were always pockets of resistance from tribes deeper within the unexplored forest. CIA agents simply could not stomp through the interior looking for plants. The loss of three research teams to date verified that.

Gibbons knew that danger came not only from the primitives and the wildlife. His Intelligence agents were tracking several research teams in approximately the same region. They were all considered hostile unless proved otherwise. The pharmaceutical industry was far more competitive than most thought and with international involvement the risks for personal safety were even greater. As Gibbons assembled his own recon team, his main concern was security. As an old football star, he knew that even the best quarterback was worthless without the protection of a good offensive line. Likewise, any science team he hired would have to be protected in order to be effective. Not knowing what to expect in the Amazon, he picked his best and brightest. Unfortunately for Gibbons, the adversaries they'd attract in the Amazon would be no match for his agents. There were dangers in Amazonia that no civilized man cold ever hope to anticipate, much less defend against. The lessons learned would haunt the colonel for the rest of his life.

Chapter 29

Agents In The Field

Agent Sutherland was covered with mosquitoes as he parted the brush. Crouched out of sight he watched and waited. He was in his sixth week of surveillance, but was confident that the batch of banisteriopsis vines nearby was the source of the ayahuasca tea that the local shamans were brewing. It was obvious from the strike marks of the bark that someone or something was sampling the vine. (field observers were somewhat surprised to learn that jaguars would occasionally sample the hallucinogen.)

The average man would have found the mosquito swarm too much to bear. The average man, however, does not survive two years of jungle guerrilla warfare in Vietnam he way Sutherland did. Hardened by his Special Forces training, and confident that antimalarial medication was protecting him, the mosquitoes were a nuisance but no real obstacle. The only real problem they caused

was their insistence on flying into and biting his eyeballs. It is hard

to concentrate one's gaze with mosquitoes on one's pupils.

Suddenly, there was movement.

About one hundred yards away, Sutherland could see the rustle

of bushes. From that distance, he couldn't determine if it was man

or beast. Either one could spell danger. After a few tense moments,

he figure of a biped emerged. Sutherland recognized him

immediately as he shaman of the nearby village. An older, sinewy

man with gray hair and skin shiny with perspiration, he displayed the

agility of a teenager. He headed straight for the sacred vines.

Although Sutherland had mustered a rudimentary understanding

of their language, he had never approached the tribe's people

directly. The risks were simply too great. Instead, he spied on their

rituals and stalked them masterfully on their own turf. The word

from headquarters was that the tea this shaman prepared was

somewhat peculiar and the CIA wanted to know more about it.

Sutherland's task was to identify and sample the plants used in the

preparation. Of course, the shaman spent much of his day collecting unusual plants, and it was hard to determine which were used for ayahuasca. Sutherland was narrowing it down. He didn't know what the CIA needed it for and he didn't care.

The shaman efficiently sliced off several pieces of bark and bundled them up. Apparently, there was a ritual order of plant collecting, and the banisteriopsis was first. As the shaman tied the bundle, Sutherland accidentally shifted his weight too far back and nearly fell from his perch. The shaman looked piercingly in his direction for what seemed like an hour, then stood and departed. Sutherland breathed a sigh of relief, cursing his own carelessness.

Following he shaman was extremely challenging. It was difficult enough to trace his path through the thick foliage and unfamiliar trails, but to do so silently was virtually impossible. He had to stay far enough back so that the inevitable branch breaking would not be heard, but obviously close enough for visual tracking. At one point the trail opened up into a clear corridor and Sutherland entered cautiously. As he made the first turn past a huge boulder he froze. Thirty yards ahead and heading directly for him was the old shaman. Thinking fast, Sutherland backed up and clumsily struggled to the top of the boulder. There he waited, not wanting to draw a

breath.

The silence was broken by the sound of running water. Puzzled,

Sutherland risked glancing over the rock. Several feet away in the

peace of the midday sun, the shaman was urinating on the boulder.

Must be some kind of ritual, Sutherland thought. It was then that he

noticed that he too had urinated, only he had done so accidentally

while still clothed.

Waiting a few moments he pressed on. So far, the shaman had

only collected one plant species, the banisteriopsis. Patience,

patience he kept telling himself. Finally, it paid off. Working his

way into the narrowed trail back into the forest he saw the shaman

crouched at a bush. After examining it thoroughly, he cut off some

leafy branches, bundled them and moved on.

Sutherland again waited, then approached the bush. It certainly

didn't look unusual, but he took samples anyway. The leaves were

small and pointed, with a smooth finish. Sutherland bit into one of

them and shuddered involuntarily at the bitter taste. He smiled.

Although no botanist, he knew that the bitterness indicated the presence of alkaloids, nitrogen based chemicals into which category most plant drugs fit. Obviously, though, it would take a sophisticated laboratory to analyze the plant. Even a trained botanical expert would be hard pressed to identify the majority of plants in the rain forest.

Sutherland pressed the sample into his plant collection kit and looked up. The sky was darkened and the impending rains would hinder his return. He estimated that he was two hours from his base. With rain that would double. He had to hurry. At least the rainstorm would rinse his soiled pants.

Several yards back, the shaman frowned. He thought he'd hard something and when he doubled back he found the white man stealing his plants right from the bush. Carefully, he pulled out one of three poison tipped arrows and unstrapped his bow. He knew the spirits would not approve of the misuse of the sacred plants and the only way to appease them would be sacrifice the perpetrator and return the plants.

Sutherland pushed on. The rain was so intense that he was completely blinded. Several times already he had strayed from his trail and had to double back. He didn't know it but each time he lost the trail he confused the warrior who was pursuing him. Finally, a clearing appeared and the canopy gave way to a misty manioc field. Checkpoint. Carefully hidden in a dense thicket was Sutherland's supply station. A two-way radio, some food rations and shotgun greeted him. When the shaman saw the shotgun he stopped. He'd seen the damage they could do to a man, and retreated. His poison arrows were no match for the fire stick. He headed back to his village to prepare the ayahuasca, wondering what the stranger would learn about his plants.

Chapter 30

Confession

" I don't imagine you'd care to explain what that was all about?" Kelly's voice was a blend of anger and sarcasm. After Bob had dragged her and John out the back of Craig's house, they quickly decided to split up and Kelly shot home. She had watched Craig's house and after a few hours when nothing else happened she decided to call him.

" I'd love to, but I haven't got a clue myself, really." Craig hoped she believed him.

" Looked awfully serious to me." She had seen Dressens dash out of the house and peel out in his van, obviously pissed off.

" Yeah. I'm hoping John can shed some light on this."

" Well, as soon as you find out I'd like you to call me. Any time."

" Deal."

" OK. I'll talk to you later." As she hung up she decided that she had no reason to doubt Craig's honesty. Assuming there was a good explanation, she figured she'd withhold any judgment until she heard the facts. In the meantime, she decided she would do the one thing that could cause a lot of trouble-telling Kyle after he returned from his conference.

" Want a beer?" she asked from the kitchen. They had just finished dinner and Kyle had adjourned to the living room for a quick glance at the newspaper while Jason played in his playpen.

" Sure," he replied, somewhat surprised. He didn't drink that much, and usually grabbed his own. She brought him his beer and sat down on the couch across the room.

" Can we talk?" she asked.

He looked up from the paper. That question was rarely a prelude to good news.   " Sure. What's up?" He quickly inventoried his mental to-do list to determine if he had forgotten one of her requests.

" I wanted to talk to you about his belly," she said, gesturing toward Jason. " I did some research at the library." She lied, holding up the information sheets on ayahuasca the guys had given her.

He took the sheets and glanced over them, a curious look creeping onto his face. He looked up at her. " Are you joining a cult?" referring to the thousands of ayahuasca devotees in South America.

She laughed. "No, nothing like that. And it's a religion, not a cult. It just sounded interesting, maybe worth looking into."

" What do you mean, looking into?" he asked, completely surprised.

" Well, you of all people should admit hat there are medical treatments that are shunned in the U.S. but are used extensively in other countries."

" Yeah. But there's a difference between alternative medicine and hallucinogenic drug use."

" Like what?" she demanded. She surprised herself with her fervent argument in favor of ayahuasca.

" Oh come on. Like there's no difference between swallowing ginseng and smoking a joint?"

" Of course there is. What's that got to do with anything?"

" Is ayahuasca a hallucinogen or not?"

" Yes. But that's not the whole…"

" Wait a minute." He stood and began pacing in front of her. " Let's assume for a second that ayahuasca has some merit, medically speaking. And let's say that we decide to try it. Then what? We cruise into some biker bar and start checking with dealers? " He began a charade. " Hey man, I need to score some ayahuasca, you holding?"

She had to smile. She could picture Kyle haggling with a drug dealer in some seedy bar over some ayahuasca. It was time to spill the beans- some of them, anyway. " I know where to get it."

He stared at her incredulously, his mind racing. Was this a joke? Or had she gone over the deep end? " OK, where?"

" Craig Hunt's friend."

" Should I know this person?"

" He's the lawyer that lives up the street."

As far as Kyle was concerned, it was a toss up as to which scenario was worse. Either his wife had lost her sanity or she was living a secret life during the day while he was at work.

" I wasn't aware you were close," he said, the suspicion hanging heavily in his voice.

" It's not like that. It's…"

" Yes?"

She shook her head. Suddenly she was sorry she'd brought it up. A tear began to form in her left eye. Compassion washed away everything else that was going through Kyle's mind. He sat down

next to her and gave her a hug.

" Hey, you can tell me anything, you know that." He smiled at

her.

She thought for a moment. The bizarre story she was about to

tell needed to be organized in her head. She had gone over the

events in her mind many times but the idea of narrating the

experience in a rational way to her husband seemed a daunting task.

" First of all, Craig and his friends are as mystified as I am," she

began. " Craig's buddy John is the ring leader. Apparently, he's

spent a lot of time in Brazil learning about medicinal plants with a

shaman."

" A shaman?" Kyle sneered.

" I think that part's a whole other story," she continued. "Just

keep in mind that these guys aren't druggies or anything. Anyway,

Craig and John and another guy, Bob, experimented a little with

ayahuasca. Apparently, when you drink it you start experiencing these visions. It's all part of the mystique surrounding the ayahuasca."

" What kind of visions?"

" I guess it varies but in some cases there's supposed to be some telepathy, and even prophesy."

" Do you buy this?"

" To some extent. I mean, you must admit there's more to every day life than meets the eye. I mean, just because our modern scientific world can't explain it, it doesn't mean that the thousands of years of ayahuasca therapy in the rain forest are a bunch of bullshit."

"I agree that we're a little close minded. But a drug that induces clairvoyance and telepathy? I think somebody's getting duped. Anyway, what's all this got to do with Jason?"

" Well, it goes back to this shaman and Craig's friend John."

" Long story."

" Right. Anyway, and this is where it gets real weird, the shaman had a vision about Jason."

" OK. Wait a minute." Kyle waved his arms in disgust.

" No, let me finish. The shaman had come to learn that unless a
life saving or miracle drug could be discovered in the rain forest
soon, the earthmovers would destroy it. The shaman's last years
would be spent searching for that drug. All along it was right under
his nose-ayahuasca. Anyway, and I admit I'm not quite clear on the
connection, he knew that ayahuasca could cure Jason."

" How does he know Jason, and how will this brew cure him?"

" The ayahuasca vision, which was triggered by John's
association with Craig." As the words came out she realized how
ridiculous it was beginning to sound.

" All right," said Kyle. " Say I'm buying all of this so far.
How's this stuff supposed to cure colic, a condition we know very
little about and one that's resisted all medical therapies for as long as
anyone can remember?"

" It's a purge."

" A purge?"

" This part was real interesting. Supposedly, the colic is caused by a microorganism that we've not yet discovered." She was careful not to include herself in the stomach pain story. " Kind of like that H. Pyle that you told about which causes ulcers."

" H. Pylori?"

" Yeah, that's it."

" So colic is caused by a microbe, not yet discovered, but which can be eradicated by ayahuasca?"

" Yeah, in a nutshell."

" Is this April first?"

" I know this sounds crazy."

" You don't don't know the half of it."

" I take it you don't buy any of it," she noted.

" No."

" Will you at least study the sheets I gave you?"

" I'll read them over, sure. But I implore you not to subject our son to this crazy scheme."

" I hope you will reconsider. What if it works?" she asked as she picked up Jason to take him to bed.

" Key word is 'if'."

She bent down to kiss him on the cheek. " Maybe you should meet with Craig and John. Anyway, we're going to bed. Coming?"

" In a minute," he said as he thumbed the ayahuasca information. He had to admit that there was something strangely plausible about the theory. After all, H. Pylori was not even suspected a few years ago in the causation of ulcers. And he had to admit also that the rain forest certainly contained countless medicinal agents. And then there those strange dreams he'd been having, so vivid and surreal that he couldn't talk about them. But what sort of microbe could cause colic? And how the hell did a shaman know about Jason? Suddenly the woman he was about to crawl into bed with seemed like a complete stranger.

As he shut off the lights and locked the door, he felt a twinge of pain in his abdomen. " No, couldn't be."

Chapter 31

Agents In The Field II

Sutherland watched the courier disappear up river. Two hours later, the boat would rendezvous with a private jet owned by Wood Pharmaceuticals, and late that night a representative from Wood's Special Biologics Division would pick up the special package at the airport. A payoff may have to take place in order to import the biologicals, but unidentified pressed plants were rarely a problem in customs. Within twenty-four hours, Roger Temple would begin the arduous task of identifying the plant's substituents. Sutherland looked up at the canopy. He hadn't slept for at least twenty hours and was looking forward to doing just that. This called for a minor celebration, and he planned on spending the morning with a pint of Wild Turkey. Tomorrow he would start over again, following the shaman and collecting his plants.

Unfortunately, the shaman had other plans for Sutherland. Watching from fifty yards away he drew a poison arrow and attached it to his bow. Watching, waiting, he knew he had only one choice. As Sutherland came within thirty yards the shaman released the arrow. Piercing Sutherland's intercostal muscles and lodging in his diaphragm, the arrow's poison began to take effect. Felled by the impact of the projectile, Sutherland found himself paralyzed. The neurotoxins had already begun to sabotage the workings of his musculature. Within seconds of the realization that he could no longer move his arms or legs, his breathing apparatus failed. Without the diaphragm to inflate his lungs, Sutherland was slowly suffocating. His mind was fully aware of his plight, and was overcome with the terror of the situation. As his ocular muscles malfunctioned, his eyes lost their ability to focus. His last vision before losing consciousness was the primitive fletching of a poison arrow against the backdrop of the now hostile jungle canopy, teeming with life forms which would soon recycle his poisoned body into the endless food chain.

Back in the safety of his lab, Temple was ready. He had checked and rechecked his equipment and had prepped two recently hired botanists to help identify the new plant specimen. In a sense, Temple was exploring uncharted territory. His entire career had been devoted to synthetic chemistry and this involved identification of naturally existing chemicals. If the botanists were able to narrow down the plant's family, they might be able to give Temple a head start on the chemical identification. He would need it.

Early on, Temple had theorized that the desired properties of ayahuasca could be traced to a single chemical entity. The main drug was believed to be a beta carboline, harmaline, but Temple's experiments with synthetic harmaline proved inconclusive. Next he pursued other plant sources containing harmaline, one of which was easier to procure than banisteriopsis. Syrian Rue was being successfully cultivated in North America and was popular with the underground Gnostics. High in harmaline content, Temple ran some preliminary experiments with the plant but again the results were inconclusive. It was becoming more and more apparent that there was a vital combination of drugs in ayahuasca that was responsible for its effects. He needed a breakthrough.

His idea for coming up with a breakthrough was best kept secret. He knew if it leaked out his job and career would be in jeopardy. He was conducting experiments on himself. Temple was a survivor of the drug soaked seventies, his teenage drug experimentation actually leading him on the path to the academic pursuit of pharmacological research. If ayahuasca enhanced human mental capabilities, then only human experimentation would prove it. He had a sinking feeling that Colonel Gibbons would secretly approve, but Temple wasn't ready to approach the top brass. No, he didn't want to deal with Gibbons any sooner than he had to.

The courier had to practically jog to keep up with Gibbons. The colonel wanted to be on hand to personally deliver the plant specimens to Temple. It had been over two weeks since their last meeting and he wanted an update. This would provide a perfect opportunity.

Gibbons had spent the morning in private meeting with Quentin Marks, the director o the CIA. The pressure was on. The initial excitement over ayahuasca was beginning to fade, and the possibility that Project R.O.N. might fail began to sink in. With the Summit rapidly approaching, it was looking grim that a mind-enhancing drug would be ready. Gibbons didn't want to put too much pressure on Temple, but he had to coax on the research a little bit. And, perhaps just as importantly, he was just plain interested in ayahuasca.

The phone in the anteroom buzzed. Temple's secretary picked it up. The message was short and to the point- the plants were here.

Temple hurried to the security door and unlocked it. As he opened the door, a swarm of butterflies began dancing in his stomach. Gibbons! *Jesus Christ, he thought. Tighten the thumbscrews.*

" Dr. Temple," said Gibbons as he glided through the door."
Hope you don't mind. Just wanted to personally deliver these
specimens." He handed the package to Temple.

The chemist took the bundle and enthusiastically took them to
his lab. Opening the wrapper, he smiled. Sutherland had
meticulously dried and pressed the specimens. Included were
leaves, branches, roots and blossoms. If the team were unable to
identify the plants it would have been no fault of the field agent. An
herbal aroma filled the air.

Gibbons leaned over to get his first look. " Looks like quality
specimens."

"Sure does. Everything's preserved beautifully," agreed
Temple. " Your man knew what he was doing."

" Sutherland. Best in the business. He's probably rounding up
another specimen as we speak." Actually Sutherland was feline
fodder, but Gibbons would never learn his fate.

Temple and his botanist associates began to spread out the
specimens. Beth Parker, a tall, red headed graduate student from

Georgetown, concentrated on the leaves. Pete Murray, an

agricultural consultant for the State of Virginia, began examining the

blossoms. Gibbons and Temple focused on the bark. Thanks to

computer graphics, the researchers could compare their specimens

against hundreds of plant photos in a matter of hours. Temple's plan

involved each team narrowing down their specimens to ten existing

plants. They would have the ten closest looking leaves, blossoms,

and bark. In a best case scenario, there would be duplicates in each

grouping of ten.

" Got any coffee?" asked an exhausted Gibbons.

" Sure, I'm ready for a break myself. Come on." Temple led

the colonel to his lounge.

" You always work until four a.m.?" asked Gibbons, removing

his tie.

" Sure, doesn't every government contract worker?" Temple

smiled as he made the coffee.

Gibbons nodded. " How many plants do you have in your file?"

" About ten thousand. But I guarantee this plant won't be in there. We'll get close, though."

" How can you be so sure?"

" There's a million species out there, but the basic families are fairly well delineated."

" So if you hit on a certain family, you'll proceed from there?"

" We're assuming that the alkaloid content will be similar in similar plants. Just like the capsaicin content in the dozens of pepper species."

" Why not go right into the chemical analysis?"

" Needle in a haystack. We need to narrow it down as much as possible. If we have some idea of what we're looking for we may have a fighting chance."

Gibbons patted him on the back. " Sounds like you know what you're doing. Anything else we can do for you?"

" Sure. You can find me some human volunteers to try this stuff once we isolate it." Temple was only half joking.

" I wish we could," lamented Gibbons. " We just can't risk a scandal."

" Certainly we're not just going to give this to the President without some human testing."

" No. When we're ready we'll get some volunteers. But we're going by the book, understand?"

" Sure, but…"

" No buts," interrupted Gibbons." I know you're enthusiastic about this, but there are a lot of interested parties here." He nodded to the lab. " Besides, there's a lot of work to be done in there before we worry about that."

" Sure, I understand." Temple sipped his coffee. Actually, he didn't understand. With or without Gibbons' blessing, Temple would conduct human experiments. His curiosity was overpowering and the lure of ayahuasca had pulled him in. As he ushered Gibbons to the door, an hour later, he assured him that the research would come to a conclusion very soon. Unfortunately, it would not come without a price.

Chapter 32

Narrow Escape

The following morning, Gibbons groggily powered up his security computer. The web, as his agents called it, had not picked up the scheduled check in message from Sutherland. Amazonia was considered a level three zone, five being the safest and one being predictably dangerous, whether from natural hazards or hostiles. According to protocol, an investigation in a level three zone would not be authorized until two check ins were missed. Sutherland was fifteen minutes from number two.

Gibbons had already lost seven agents in the last twelve months. He could scarcely afford to lose Sutherland. He looked at his watch. Five more minutes. He stood and walked over to the map of South

America on his wall. The pins that were stuck into the map near the Amazon roughly designated Sutherland's territory. He could be anywhere.

Exactly one hour past check in time, Gibbons picked up the phone. They'd lost another. He dialed his reconnaissance commander, Gilbert Evans.

" Evans."

" Gil, this is Gibbons."

" Looks like we've got trouble."

" I was hoping you'd picked up something down there." Although Gibbons' master computer pulled information from all worldwide stations, it was Evans who could fine-tune an otherwise weak transmission, or perhaps an unusual wavelength emanating from damaged or foreign equipment. If Evans didn't pick up a message, then chances were that no message was sent.

" Sorry. Sixty-three minutes overdue. We're ready to mobilize on your command."

"Go. And Gil," he paused. " Be careful."

" Understood. We'll give hourly updates upon arrival."

As Gibbons hung up he made a decision that for him took an unusually long time to make. Standard procedure was out the door. Search warrants and surveillance had netted exactly nothing and his patience was gone. Six weeks had passed and they were no closer to the source of the unusual ayahuasca blend. For a self-proclaimed man of action, waiting was not an option.

He picked up the intercom. " This is Gibbons. Bring my car around." He smiled. He was going to pay a personal visit to one John Masters. He had avoided direct confrontation so as not to induce John to flee. But now his options had run out. Besides, he'd use a carrot rather than a stick. He was ready to make John an offer he couldn't refuse. CIA style.

Gibbons had remarkably liberal views on the drug issue. In fact,

he favored legalization in view of the decades of futile interdiction

policies. He knew that human nature and the need for the pursuit of

artificial paradise would create an overpowering demand for drugs.

Human beings would never exist on planet earth without mind-

altering drugs. As an avid martini and cigar man, Gibbons

understood well the concept of altered states. And he was open

minded enough to accept that not all drugs were evil when used with

maturity and common sense. No, he didn't condone the use of

cocaine in the inner cities. But if LSD could help unlock the hidden

tangles of a psychiatric patient's mind, then more power to them.

En route to John Master's home, Gibbons realized how much he

missed fieldwork. His wife of twenty two years had passed away a

few years ago-undiagnosed breast cancer-and he poured all of his

energy into his work. Ironically, now that he was free from family

obligations, he was too old to be chasing thugs and hopping fences.

Or so he thought. He didn't know it, but in a short time he would try

to invade the tropical rain forest in search of an as yet undiscovered

plant drug. Undiscovered by white man, that is, for it had been in use for centuries in Amazonia. His hunch was that Masters was probably the only hope Gibbons had. As the plane landed, Gibbons psyched himself up for the meeting. He wondered how persuasive he could still be.

He had arranged a car to pick him up at the airport and transport him directly to Master's home. Of course, it was chancy whether John would actually be there. If he wasn't, Gibbons had search warrant in hand. The feds can search a home with or without the suspect present. After a forty five-minute drive, he arrived in front of the apartment.

" Better come along. I'm not as young as I used to be," he said to McCoy, his driver.

" Yes sir," came the deadpan reply.

Masters lived in an unpretentious, one-bedroom apartment in a sprawling complex. Gibbons approached his unit and rang the doorbell, which apparently didn't work. He knocked, waited a few seconds, knocked again, then turned to McCoy.

" Open it."

" Right away, colonel." After a few seconds the door opened, creating an entrance to the laboratory of a shaman's apprentice. After a quick check, Gibbons concluded hat Masters wasn't home.

" Watch the door," he motioned to the front door. Putting his gun away, he looked around the apartment. It was clean but cluttered and smelt of incense. Numerous artifacts from John's travels were carefully displayed throughout the apartment. Gibbons wasn't quite sure what he was looking for, but began opening drawers and cupboards. There was nothing peculiar, let alone illegal. He was about to enter the bedroom when McCoy alerted him.

" Sir, I believe the suspect has arrived."

" Keep the door locked."

Gibbons glanced into the bedroom. The bed was neatly made and the room was more cluttered than the living room. On the dresser was an object that caught Gibbons' attention. It was a jar with a trace of liquid in the bottom. Quickly, Gibbons picked it up and smelled the contents, which made his eyes roll. He screwed back the lid and replaced it on the dresser in anticipation of Masters'

arrival. Had he looked in John's closet he would have discovered

the very object of his search.

He made his way back to the hallway and glanced at McCoy,

who had pulled his gun. Gesturing to the gun and shaking his head,

Gibbons signaled that there was probably no threat of violence. He

doubted that Masters was either armed or violent. His plan was to

use reason over force, and he was a very persuasive man. The sound

of keys was followed by a click of the deadbolt.

John had been job hunting all morning and had come home for

lunch before resuming his errands. He sensed something was amiss.

Reacting quickly, he was gone. Calculating that there'd be no time

to get into his car he ran like hell.

" God Dammit," shouted Gibbons as they took off. Trying to

keep up with Masters and McCoy he guessed he'd be good for one

hundred yards. Thirty yards later he pulled up with a cramp.

Jumping fences and shooting through familiar terrain, John was

easily able to lose his assailants. Finding safe haven in a nearby

garage, he quickly checked his jean pocket. The glass vial was intact. The question, of course, was who the hell was after him.

Like it or not, he would soon find out.

Chapter 33

Swenson's Plan

It could be argued that Malcolm Swenson is too smart for

himself. What began as a disturbing dream culminated in a full

day's worth of meetings, and the conclusion he reached would

transform his career and the future of Wood Pharmaceuticals. Soon after receiving Temple's research notes, Swenson's medicinal

chemistry background exploded to the surface. He had found a flaw

in Temple's thinking, and after double and triple checking his

theory, he was sure that Temple's research had unlocked the answer,

yet apparently the researcher hadn't realized it himself. Not sure of

the correct course of action, Swenson decided to sleep on it. His

dream saw him initiating an independent research effort based on his

newly discovered theory, and his lawyers had confirmed the legal

immunity involved. In other words, there was nothing stopping

Swenson from pursuing a new research project based on Temple's

research.

Naturally it was inherently risky to oppose the CIA account, let

alone because of a dream. The fact of the matter was that he had a

tremendous amount of respect for both Temple and Gibbons. He

was sure that if Temple had read the research at this point, it was

doubtful he'd go back and find it later. Swenson, it would appear,

had simply assigned independent research money for a similar

project. Neither the CIA nor Temple would have any clue. In fact,

he'd still encourage the Temple team, for Wood would still benefit from any breakthroughs. Now, however, he could directly control his own research team, doubling his chances of successful research and development.

After meeting with Quentin Milburn, the corporate attorney who verified the legal implications, Swenson brought in James Keyworth, one of the senior research chemists at Wood.

Keyworth was s slight, frail man of sixty-two. His twenty-eight years at Wood had produced over two hundred patents, twelve of which had positive commercial results. Swenson didn't care for him personally, but his professional skills were unequaled. He was Wood's home run hitter.

" Jim. Thanks for stopping in."

" Sure Malcolm. What would I do, refuse?" Swenson remembered quickly why he didn't care for Keyworth's sarcastic manner.

"Anyway, there's something I wanted to consult with you about." Swenson paused, trying to recreate his rehearsed presentation. His primary concern was secrecy. He wanted no leaks, and in no way wanted Keyworth to make the connection between this proposal and Temple's research. "I'd like to pursue the possibilities in the Alzheimer's arena. My market research tells me that there's probably no more profitable and altruistic category in medicinal research."

At the sound of the words profitable and altruistic mentioned in the same sentence, Keyworth's eyebrows furrowed his brow. He said nothing, waiting for Swenson to continue.

Swenson, on the other hand, waited for Keyworth to comment. " Well?"

" Challenging, to say the least. I wouldn't really know where to begin."

" I do," Swenson said confidently. " Look at this." He handed Keyworth a brief workup of his theory.

Keyworth studied the research proposal, reading and rereading the key points. Suddenly his sarcasm was gone. " This is nothing short of incredible."

Swenson smiled. He was afraid that no other chemist would appreciate his theory. " Does it make sense?" he asked, knowing full well that it did.

" In general, the theory is sound. Revolutionary, but sound. I'd like to study this for a few days and test the viability."

" That's great. That's what I was hoping you'd say." Swenson had difficulty controlling his enthusiasm. " I had always doubted the future of the single receptor theories."

" I still see some trouble spots."

" What, for example?"

" Well, for starters, neural regeneration has always been suspect. How can we get around that?"

" I've received some classified research information that introduces an herbal drug from South America that shows promise," he said, dodging the specifics. " I'll tell you more when time allows."

" I'd like to see…"

" Please," said Swenson, putting up his hand. " I've hardly gathered all the facts myself."

" Sure. Can I keep this?" Keyworth asked, holding up the folder.

" It's for your eyes only."

" Understood."

" Good. Call me when you want to brainstorm on this."

" I will. Thank you." Keyworth shook Swenson's hand as he stood.

" And Jim. This is completely classified."

" Yes, you made that clear." He turned and left.

Swenson had a few minutes before his next appointment. So far, so good. His next meeting would be the key, the make it or break it point. He had called Marty Preston, an ethnopharmacologist with a Harvard background. Swenson knew that part of Temple's delays were due to the CIA's inability to procure enough raw material for research. He was confident that Preston could get down to Brazil, acquire the necessary ayahuasca samples, and provide an efficient and reliable source of raw materials. The only issue was money. Preston wouldn't come cheap.

Marty Preston was a well-preserved forty-year-old. He was a botanical mercenary, with an uncanny ability to infiltrate the deepest forests of the tropics and study the plants and their uses. He held great reverence for the rain forest but had no problem earning a substantial living by raiding its natural treasures.

Their meeting was short and sweet. Swenson showed Preston photos of the plant samples he needed, and Preston named his price. They haggled a little. Swenson didn't say what he needed them for, and Preston didn't ask.

" When do you need this?"

" ASAP."

" I can leave tomorrow, spend a few weeks searching, back by the end of the month."

" Deal." Swenson nervously shook his hand. The price was high, $100,000, but the payoff was potentially huge. He had set the wheels in motion. Swenson had entered a race that was full of pitfalls and doubt, but which would force him to the forefront of

medical research. There was no turning back now.

Chapter 34

Tragic Trip

Tom Stewart eyed the brackish fluid nervously, then drank it quickly. The resultant taste in his mouth was indescribable. By itself, the ayahuasca is incredibly unpalatable. But combining that with the aftertaste of wine and cheese from his afternoon snack gave Tom an almost overwhelming urge to vomit all over Roger Temple's coffee table. Fighting the growing nausea, Tom found himself struggling to swallow the saliva that was being forced into his mouth by a digestive system under attack. Sweating profusely, his face lost all color. Temple, who'd never experienced such a reaction in four previous ayahuasca sessions, looked on with concern. If Stewart vomited, his experiment would abruptly end before it began.

"You going to be OK?" he asked his assistant.

Closing his eyes and swallowing, Stewart looked up. " Whew. That's nasty stuff."

" Could be why it never caught on in this country."

" Could be," Stewart said as he got up to walk around. Temple had warned him about the nausea from ayahuasca, but it was much worse than he expected.

Temple watched him anxiously. He wondered if it had something to do with what Stewart had eaten. He had advised him to eat lightly if at all and hoped Stewart had taken his advice. After a few laps around the family room, Stewart sat back down.

" I think I'll be all right, unless it comes back. The nausea, I mean."

" It shouldn't. Once the visions kick in you should be fine," Temple reassured him. " Just sit back and relax."

Forty minutes later, Stewart was passing his hands in front of his face, noting the "trails" they left in their wake. He was thoroughly enjoying the sensation. Looking across the room, he noticed that Temple was fully reclined, eyes closed, enjoying his own ayahuasca experience. However, within seconds, the image of his boss transformed into that of a large cat, a jaguar. Stewart closed his eyes and reopened them to find the cat was still there. He was amazed. Transfixed on the vision, Stewart watched as several immense green snakes slithered out of the jaguar's mouth and onto the floor.

Reflexively, he lifted his feet. Shutting his eyes he was treated to a

phenomenal display of light and color, wild animals and geometrical

shapes. Unfortunately, he was overcome by waves of nausea, and

opened his eyes in desperation. The jaguar was gone, and Temple

was back in the chair, looking at him. Stewart smiled and Temple

returned the gesture, his teeth shining like an ivory beacon.

Stewart wanted to speak, but couldn't. As he watched Temple,

he struggled to keep his eyes open, but they shut as though they were

weighted down. He began to fly. He found himself cruising over a

lush landscape, his body turning at will. It was dreamlike but he was

fully cognizant. He passed over a variety of living beings, some

human, some animal, some unknown. It was pleasant, but somewhat

frightening.

Suddenly, he was overcome by a feeling of intense nausea.

After taking several deep breaths, which helped a little, he staggered

to Temple's bathroom. There he retched for what seemed like hours.

His stomach was practically empty except for a little ayahuasca.

Therefore, the esophageal spasms were dry heaves, which racked his body mercilessly. The combined after taste of ayahuasca and cheese further stimulated the gut wrenching nausea. Finally, mercifully, his episode came to an end. He sat on the bathroom floor, dazed, sore and fully in the throes of a major hallucinogenic experience.

Roger Temple's eyes were closed when Stewart left the room. As he opened them he realized the absence of his associate. Just as he summoned the energy to initiate a search, Stewart stumbled back into his chair, visibly shaken.

" You OK?" Temple asked.

Stewart looked at him, trying to connect the sounds of spoken language to the image before him. He couldn't and merely stared blankly. He was miserable. Closing his eyes helped, and before long the nausea was replaced by feelings of total bliss. Soon, his mind's eye was treated to a visual display that was breathtakingly beautiful. It was as if he had been transported bodily to the rain forest floor, surrounded by the most powerfully exquisite foliage he had ever imagined. The visual display was accompanied by intense olfactory and tactile sensations that gave him the very real impression that he was actually there. His movements were very fluid, like floating rather than walking, and he came across an area that seemed to be a final destination. There, in a large grove, was a batch of identical plants. He couldn't identify them, but they looked familiar. He began to explore the area and soon realized that the entire forest in that region contained only that one plant.

Suddenly, a figure appeared in the vision. It was an archetypal figure of an ancient medicine man. He was primitively clad, with graying hair and piercing eyes. Without speaking, he held up one of the plants and informed Stewart that these were the plants he was searching for. He then disappeared, leaving the startled botanist alone in the forest. He opened his eyes

Temple appeared statuesque, having not budged for quite some time. Glancing to his left Stewart noticed a pad of paper and pen on the phone stand. Without thinking, he reached for the paper and began sketching the plant in his vision. Not being an artist, he was amazed at the proficiency he exhibited in drawing the minute details of the unknown plant, including the bark, leaves and flowers. When he had finished, he had produced an amazingly detailed rendition of a plant whose identity was unknown. He then realized what happened. Excitedly, he screamed at Temple. The shaman in his

vision had given him the answer to their " mystery" ayahuasca

ingredient!

Temple opened his eyes in response to Stewart's scream. He

couldn't figure out why, but his associate was frantically waving a

plant sketch at him. Stewart's excitement was short lived, however.

As abruptly as his tirade started, he dropped the sketchpad and

dropped his head into his hands. Temple looked on curiously, trying

to figure out what was going on with Stewart. It appeared that his

associate was in a great deal of pain.

In fact, it was the most excruciating pain he had ever

experienced. His head felt like something inside had exploded. At

the instant the pain hit, his world went black. His eyes no longer

functioned, and the pain inside his skull increased relentlessly. His

visions of death ensued, and mercifully, death came swiftly. The

agony was too much to bear. He slumped in his chair, a stream of

blood running from his right nostril.

Temple tried in vain to make the vision go away. Buzz kill.

The image of his one time associate, gripped by death with the grimace of mortal pain, became too real. His friend was dead, perhaps due to the tea, making Temple responsible. He tried haplessly to move, wanting to help Stewart in any way he could. But he was helpless. He settled back in his chair, a prisoner of his hallucinogenic haze. A nightmare had become reality.

Chapter 35

John Lays Low

" Goddammit," Craig yelled as he bolted for the stove, his pasta boiling over. Removing it from he burner and turning to his sink, he did a double take. There was a man climbing out of the ravine behind his house.

" What the hell…" Craig set the pasta in the sink and went over to his sliding doors. As the man ascended the hill, Craig realized it was John. He jumped up to the deck where Craig greeted him.

" What's going on?" Craig asked.

John practically pushed him out of the way, slammed the door shut and ran to a corner of the kitchen where he'd be out of sight.

He held his finger up to his lips, signaling Craig to shut up.

Deciding to play the game, Craig went back to the sink, pretending

to work on the pasta, which by now was unfit for a soup line.

" I'm not sure if I'm being followed. Keep your eyes peeled,"

John whispered.

Craig's mind was racing. The combination of excitement and

fear was exhilarating. One thing was sure- he wasn't hungry any

more. He looked out toward the ravine and saw nothing, then

glanced back at his friend, crouched in the corner.

" Anyone in particular I should be on the lookout for?"

" I guess there's nothing to worry about," said John as he got

up. " Sorry."

" What's going on, if you don't mind my asking?"

" No, you may ask." John was looking in the sink. " Jesus,

what a train wreck. Got anything edible?"

" Overcooked," said Craig, motioning to the pasta.

" No kidding."

Craig went to the refrigerator and pulled out two beers. " I'm all ears."

John popped open his beer and took a long swig. " CIA, I believe."

Craig had assumed some branch of law enforcement, most likely undercover city or county agents. He wasn't happy to admit it, but even the DEA entered his mind. But certainly not the CIA. " CIA? What the fuck would they be doing with us?"

" Us? Or me?"

" Well, whomever." Craig looked piercingly at his longtime friend. " What are you involved in, anyway?"

" Believe me, nothing more than what I've told you."

" Then why are you imagining that the CIA is following you?"

" I had a strange meeting in Sao Paolo last year. I didn't mention it because I've never really believed it. Until now."

" What kind of meeting?"

" It was a chance run in, actually, with a friend of mine. A Brazilian policeman. He told me there'd been some US agents snooping around. Specifically, they were looking for an American smuggling drugs out of the Mubawe region, which was where Bitu's tribe is. He told me to watch my step."

" He's on the level?"

" Yeah, if by that you mean he was on my side."

" Well, yeah. I mean in a foreign country it would be hard to trust anybody."

" I know. I'm always careful. That's why his warning caught me off guard."

" Did he know that you were bringing ayahuasca to the states?" Craig asked.

John paused. " He's my shipping contact."

" You fall, he falls."

" Possibly. Anyway, any time the US feds go down, it's trouble for the nationals. They don't care for the snooping."

" So you kept shipping anyway?"

" Oh yeah. We were discreet, but we kept it going. Don't forget, I was taking small amounts for personal use. Others were actually smuggling. The network is quite extensive."

" The network?"

" Ayahuasca is catching on my friend."

" You mean as a street drug?"

" No. Never. I'm talking about a few tight circles of 'tea' drinkers who are exploring the spiritual aspects of the ayahuasca. It's not a stoner's game."

" So why is the CIA worried about it?"

" This is all hearsay, rumors, all unsubstantiated," John began. " The CIA is into some weird shit. Supposedly there's some serious research going on."

" Like what?"

" Mind enhancement."

" Not surprising. Didn't they do a lot research on LSD and psylocibin?"

" Still do. Ayahuasca is a little different because it's never been a popular street drug. It's harder to get."

" That's where you come in."

" I guess. At least that's the only thing I can think of. Believe me, I wouldn't have dragged you guys into this if I had any inkling."

" Kelly's scared shitless," Craig said.

" Is she out?"

" Not necessarily. She's willing to hear our explanation. Apparently she's still willing to accept the theory that ayahuasca will cure Jason and her," Craig said.

" And what do you think?"

" She wants the truth, plain and simple."

" And if she balks?' John asked.

" Such is life. We can't force her and I don't want to mislead her." Craig reached for his beer. " So where do we go from here?"

" Business as usual. I'd like to lay low for a few days. Is that cool?"

" Here? Yeah, I don't see why not." Craig paused. " You haven't been charged with anything, so you're not really a fugitive."

" Gee. Thanks for taking that into consideration."

" I'm sorry. Just my law brain sorting it out."

" What's the matter, you don't want to be an accomplice to a known fugitive?"

" Shut up asshole. Have another beer."

John accepted the offer, taking his shoes off and settling into Craig's easy chair.

" Aren't you scared?" Craig asked.

" Well the way I see it is, if they wanted me bad enough, they'd have nabbed me. I think they're watching and waiting. I think they need me."

" For what?"

" I'm not sure. But I can't wait to find out. At this point in my life, I'm ready for a little action. I've got nothing to lose, you know?"

Chapter 36

Sobering Experience

It was the most horrifying event in Roger Temple's life. Profoundly intoxicated by one of the most powerful drugs known to mankind, he struggled to control his conscious mind in an effort to help his stricken colleague who lay comatose, possibly dead, just a few short feet away. Even in a completely sober state, the crisis would have been difficult for Temple to deal with. Intoxicated, he was helpless.

He shut his eyes and tried to will himself sober, like the drunk who knows he must drive home. Unfortunately, shutting his eyes had the immediate effect of producing an incredible visual display. At times, the hallucinations were so powerful as to create doubt as to the reality of the situation. Temple's thin shred of rationality was hoping that it was all a bad illusion, one that would dissipate as his body metabolized the drug.

But it would simply not go away. Stewart's body had not budged, although now all color was gone and the once crimson stream of blood trickling from his nose had darkened and dried. Eventually, and the elapsed time was unclear, Temple was able to stand and walk over to Stewart. He was dead, no doubt about it. The autopsy would reveal a massive hemorrhagic stroke, much rarer than the occlusive type in which a clogged artery cuts off blood to the brain. There is rarely anything that can be done, save for radical brain surgery, which must be performed quickly. Stewart would get no such treatment, nor would it have helped.

His death was tragic and the coroner's ruling that it was natural causes absolved Temple of any wrongdoing. However, the symbolism of his demise once the circumstances were revealed made Stewart a martyr for a cause that was gaining momentum worldwide. The implications of a death caused by ayahuasca profoundly affected research in that arena. Even after the pieces of the puzzle were in place, Stewart's death changed the course of all research on ayahuasca.

As the effects of the tea began to wear off, Temple moved into action. He quickly cleaned up all traces of the ayahuasca, having decided to withhold that valuable piece of information from the authorities. Then he dialed 911.

" 911 Emergency."

" I need an ambulance."

" Has there been an accident?"

" My friend passed out. I think he's dead."

" Where are you now?"

" 900 West Main street. Apartment 212."

" We'll send a crew right away."

As Temple hung up he looked at his friend. He had known Stewart for four years and their friendship had survived the rigors of many difficult research assignments. He was still not convinced that the ayahuasca was responsible for what had happened. He would research that for himself. Not that it mattered. How could he not blame it on the ayahuasca?

Within ten minutes, the EMS crew arrived. As suspected, Stewart was pronounced dead. The cause death was later determined by the autopsy to be a massive cerebral hemorrhage, caused by a congenital abnormality. As far as the coroner was concerned, trauma or foul play did not cause the stroke. The blood vessel in Stewart's head was a time bomb, ready to explode at any moment.

" I'm terribly sorry, Roger." Swenson was sincerely apologetic

over the phone. " I know you were close, and by all reports Stewart

was a model employee."

" Yes. It's been a difficult couple of days," Temple said.

" Take all he time you need. The research can wait a few

days." Swenson knew that Temple wouldn't be very efficient

anyway.

" Thank you."

Swenson hung up the phone and shook his head in disbelief. He

had planned on removing Temple from the project at the end of the

month. The research was simply not getting anywhere, and he had

interviewed several other chemists who were interested in

completing the project. Now it would seem unfair. He would wait it

out a few days before making any decisions.

A few days later, Temple's conscience got the best of him, and

Swenson's job got easier. Temple's confession took the heat off

Swenson, and the sketches that Stewart made from his visions would provide the valuable piece of information that Swenson needed to complete the research.

Temple's point of view was slightly different, of course. He knew that Swenson was more concerned with outcomes than processes. He had always believed that the method was irrelevant as long as the results were achieved. Success at any cost was the unwritten motto. Therefore, he decided to take the chance that Swenson would ignore the indiscretions that let to the answer. If Stewart's mystery plant sketch proved to be the answer, then the ayahuasca episode would be forgotten. Unfortunately, Swenson didn't see it that way.

Temple had been studying plant identification files with a vengeance. Stewart's sketch was incredibly detailed and within a few days Temple had four very good candidates. Narrowed down that far, he felt he had enough ammunition to confront Swenson with his incredible account. He hoped that Swenson would agree to sponsor a junket to the Amazon, where Temple could search for the mystery plant. Hopefully, Stewart's death would not have been completely in vain. His plant sketch could help provide the answer to a problem whose solution could profoundly alter the course of human history. With or without Swenson's blessing, Roger Temple was headed for the Amazon.

Chapter 37

Testing the Theory

" Dr. Moorehead will see you now." The receptionist escorted Kyle to the back examination room. Kyle smiled at the children's decorations. Such a different atmosphere compared to his sterile examination rooms. A few minutes later, Dr. Moorehead entered.

" Dr. Ferguson, how are you?" Moorehead offered a handshake, which Kyle accepted.

" Fine, thank you. I appreciate your taking the time to see me."

" My pleasure. What can I do for you?"

" This is a little off the wall, but I wanted your opinion. It's about Kelly and Jason."

" I figured as much," said Moorehead.

" Kelly has mentioned an unusual theory and I wanted your opinion. I've never heard of it but maybe you have."

" Fire away."

" A friend of hers mentioned an herbal drug from the Amazon called ayahuasca." He deliberately left out the details about the shaman.

" I've heard of it, but I'm not familiar with it. I know it's widely used in South America as a purgative and as a catalyst for visions, conjuring up spirits, that sort of thing."

" You've heard of it used as a purgative?"

" Yes, I have, although I understand it causes vomiting, which may be interpreted as a purgative."

" Is it possible that a drug like that could wipe out a colony of unwanted bacteria in the gut?"

" I suppose. What strain of bacteria are you referring to?"

" I don't know for sure," Kyle admitted.

Moorehead looked confused. " Kyle, what are you getting at?"

" Let's suppose, hypothetically, that there's a whole subset of the population whose stomach pain is caused by an unknown bacterium?"

" You man like H. Pylori?"

" Exactly. Only instead of causing duodenal ulcers, this bacterium causes cramping in adults and..."

" And?"

" Colic in babies," Kyle said, rather weakly.

Moorehead's eyebrows shot straight through the ceiling. " Interesting theory." He stroked his well-trimmed gray beard thoughtfully.

" This bacterium," Kyle continued," would be resistant to conventional antibiotic therapy, but would be eradicated by a purgative like ayahuasca."

" Where on earth did you come up with this theory?"

" It's a long story, and the details aren't very clear to me yet. What I wanted to do was throw out my theory to you and get your opinion."

Moorehead stopped to think it over. " Theoretically, your scenario makes some sense. First of all, I believe that many diseases are caused by previously unknown bacteria and viruses. We've been bombarded recently with research that points to viral cancers and so forth. It's reasonable to postulate that colic could be a bacterial affliction. Secondly, the use of purgatives has a long history worldwide, and it's gaining popularity nowadays. Put those ideas together and it gets very interesting. Of course, there's only one way to test the theory. Ayahuasca doesn't seem like a substance that's easy to come by."

" We may have that problem licked," said Kyle.

" Is that right?"

" Yeah. Apparently Kelly knows somebody who can supply it for us."

" Very interesting, to say the least."

" Do you think it's worth a try?" Kyle asked.

" It sounds too dangerous."

" I agree, but the rewards, well. You get the picture."

" This supplier, is it anyone you can trust?" asked Moorehead.

" Actually, I don't know them personally."

" In that case I'd be very reluctant." Moorehead shook his head. " From what I remember, this ayahuasca is not something to play around with."

" Is there any way to research it?"

" There's very little research that I'm aware of. I worked with a Brazilian doctor who taught me a little about it. It came up in conversation one day."

" Is there any way I can contact him?"

" Her. Carol Vasquez. She works at the VA these days. She might be willing to help."

" Thank you. You've been a big help," Kyle said as he shook Moorehead's hand.

" I don't know about that. Please be careful. You're exploring uncharted territory here."

" You can say that again."

Kyle debated whether to go directly to the VA hospital or call first. He decided on the latter. The VA hospital was twenty miles east of town and it was already past four. He decided instead to go to the library and find out what he could. For some reason, the more he thought about ayahuasca, the more intrigued he became. The theory seemed more plausible as time progressed. His main concern was safety. If ayahuasca caused any reactions, he wondered what they were. How dangerous could this stuff be, anyway, he thought?

Chapter 38

The NSC

Charlton McCloud peered out of the window of his private helicopter. The noise of the rotor was in stark contrast to the serene beauty of the rain forest below. Shortly, the velvet canopy would surrender to the encroachment of oil fields. There was a war going on, and he wanted to stop it.

McCloud was a second generation member of the National Security Coalition, a secretive and powerful group of industrialists, retired military officers and politicians whose existence was virtually unknown to the general public who supposedly benefited most from its activities. The CIA was aware of the NSC, and in some instances worked closely with it. The conservation of the rain forest, for example, represented a common goal.

The NSC was founded in 1949, a post war invention of oil magnate J.T. Welton. Originally it consisted of six members whose wealth was not enough to satisfy their thirst for life. They wanted to be the architects of a New World order and they felt they had many of the answers. In time, the coalition grew to twenty-one members, then deflated to twelve, its present number. Their activities were all legal and peaceful. One offshoot of their policy making, for example, was the formation of large land buying groups whose sole intent was the protection of unspoiled wildernesses. Their research teams sponsored the construction of various energy saving devices, most notably involving solar and electrical energy. Much strife of the post World War II era centered on the various strategically important oil fields. Whether in the Middle East, Alaska, South America or anywhere offshore, oil production was an environmental albatross. The NSC realized that human reliance on petroleum was rapidly destroying planet earth and yet solutions were slow to develop. The NSC was trying to speed up the process.

The coalition was also interested in the rain forest for another reason, although protecting it from oil companies was commendable enough. The intellectuals of the NSC were also concerned with drug abuse. They had two goals in mind when studying the rain forest. Number one was an attempt to study drug use within cultures who apparently had woven drug use into their normal fabric of existence without ill effects to either the individual or society. Secondly, the very real threat of a society brainwashed by drugs was too real to ignore. It was chemical warfare, and the implications were frightening. With the discovery of LSD in 1938, for example, came the horrifying possibility that a community's water supply, as an example, could be laced with mind altering drugs. The fore thinking members of the NSC were well aware of the implications of such a concept in the hands of an international terrorist. What if a drug similar to LSD could be manufactured in gas form and exposed to large communities? The NSC wanted to learn about drugs before terrorists did in order to counteract such an incident, long before such acts of terrorism became commonplace.

Bold endeavors, for sure, but the NSC was well funded and very energetic. McCloud's father Victor was the first NSC member to explore the upper Amazon, and his experiences were recounted in vivid detail to his colleagues. Apparently, the drugs used in South America were far more powerful than anything seen in the States. As the oil companies invested more and more money in the area, it became clear to the NSC that something drastic was in order. There was simply too much real estate to purchase outright and ownership wouldn't guarantee preservation, for there would not be enough boundary enforcement to make it work. No, the coalition was looking for a more creative answer, and in 1978 Charlton McCloud came up with it.

The drug industry was booming and always in search of new pharmaceuticals. They also had a lot of money to invest in research and development. McCloud surmised that the drug manufacturers would be very interested in a systematic study of the plants of the rain forest. There had always been small scale research in that area, but McCloud was proposing a full scale effort to screen as many plants as possible for medicinal uses. The most difficult aspect of such an endeavor would be to convince the natives that such a project would be in their favor. McCloud envisioned an environmentally friendly battle as each drug company tried to claim its share of the forest for plant study. Promising drugs would either be synthesized or cultivated in greenhouses thereby preserving their natural habitat. Soon, however, unforeseen problems began to erode the mission.

The natives were far less hospitable than McCloud imagined. They didn't trust the gringos, regardless of intentions. Without the aid of local plant "experts" the botanists who traveled to the region were left with the formidable task of random plant screenings, the feasibility of which was questionable. By 1982, six of the original ten pharmaceutical houses had given up on the research, having found no promising medicinals.

McCloud's brainstorm, at first embraced by the ambitious pharmaceutical researchers, began to backfire. Several teams were lost and the insects and other natural hazards began to suffocate the missions. In 1984, the final research team pulled out, empty-handed. Ironically, the natives had begun to appreciate the effort. They had come to realize that there had been little or no encroachment by the oil companies in the areas that had been designated as research areas. It was not a condition based on forceful intervention, but rather public relations. The word had gotten out in the states that huge areas of Brazilian rain forest were being preserved thanks to the efforts of drug researchers. The oil companies were keenly aware that the negative publicity relating to their exploration of the forest would adversely affect their bottom line. Reluctantly, they yielded

to the pressures from environmentalists and the scientific

community.

In the meantime, McCloud became obsessed with studying the

plant drugs of the Amazon. Like Gordon Wasson, the financier

turned mycologist who traveled the world studying psychoactive

mushrooms, McCloud followed in his father's footsteps. He began

to personally travel into the forest, befriending the local medicine

men and studying their plethora of medicinally active plants. The

one that grabbed his attention was ayahuasca. During one vision, he

was informed by an inner voice that his father was sick. McCloud

flew home as soon as he could arrange it, and sure enough, his father

had been hospitalized with pneumonia. That was all the evidence

McCloud needed. The NSC had always kept a finger on the pulse of

the CIA's distant viewing and parapsychology research. This drug

would fit nicely into that experiment. It was McCloud who had

encouraged his old friend, Colonel Gibbons, to study the ayahuasca

phenomenon. Secretly, however, McCloud and his NSC team were

working toward the same goal, that of determining the true nature of ayahuasca's effects. While Gibbons was struggling to obtain

samples, McCloud was personally exploring the region, befriending

the natives and learning first hand about the ayahuasca. The missing

element was a medicinal chemist familiar with the chemicals

isolated from the tea and who had national security clearance. The

foremost researcher was a man named Temple, who was working

under contract with the CIA and Wood Pharmaceuticals. Somehow

McCloud needed to lure Temple away from that project and into his.

Unfortunately, he didn't want to step on Gibbons' toes. He needed a

break, and would soon get one.

Chapter 39

The Good Doctor Gives In

Kyle couldn't stop daydreaming. He had never fancied himself

a researcher, but after reading about the discovery of H. Pylori's role

in ulcers and the impact that those doctors had on the world's health

leadership, Kyle envisioned the rewards that would come from such

a discovery. Could ayahuasca actually solve the problem of infant

colic? He was beginning to seriously evaluate that possibility. The fantasy was becoming rather enticing- " Dr. Kyle Ferguson, discoverer of the cure for infant colic". The phone shattered his reverie.

" Dr. Ferguson."

" Hi honey."

" Hi Kelly. What's up?"

" I was just wondering if you'd given any thought to the ayahuasca experiment."

Most men get calls to remind them to bring home milk.

" Yeah, in fact I was going to call you later." It was as if she'd been reading his mind. " I'd like to meet with your friends."

" Oh Kyle. Thank you."

" Don't get too excited. I'm not sold yet, but I owe it to you to see what this is all about."

" I'll call Craig and set it up. I love you!" She hung up before he could say anything.

John was reading the paper, relaxing in exile when Craig's phone rang. He ignored it, waiting for the answering machine to handle the situation.

" Hi. You've reached 433-0110. Sorry, but Mr. Hunt, Attorney at Law, can't come to the phone right now. Please leave your message with the date and time at the beep."

How egotistical, John thought.

" Hi Craig. This is Kelly. It's Tuesday morning, around ten. It's important that you call me. I've got good news."

John debated whether to call Craig at work with that message, but decided to wait until he came home. With all the excitement, he'd almost forgotten that Kelly had agreed to take part in the experiment. Luckily, he had enough ayahuasca stashed away for one more session. For obvious reasons, he had no more shipments scheduled for awhile.

Craig arrived home shortly after five. John gestured toward the answering machine.

" Let's see what she wants," Craig said as he dialed.

" Hello?" Kelly's voice was calm despite the crying baby in the background.

" Hi Kelly. This is Craig." He wasn't sure if she recognized his voice yet.

" Oh hi. Good news. At least I think it is. Kyle has agreed to go along with the experiment, if it's still on."

" I think it is. Hold on, John is right here." He cupped the phone. " Her doc hubby said he'd go along with it. Are we still on?"

" Sure, I think everything's settled down."

" When's good?" Craig asked.

" How about Friday?" Kelly asked.

" Friday?" he asked John, who nodded. " Friday night it is."

" Can we stop by so Kyle can meet you guys first?"

" Sure, anytime."

" How about in a few hours?" she asked.

" Great."

" Ok. See you then."

Craig hung up and slapped John on the back. " We're on. They're coming by tonight for a get acquainted session."

" Cool. Guess I should shower and shave."

" Yeah, wish you would," said Craig, rolling his eyes.

The Fergusons rang the doorbell at seven o'clock. Craig had just finished the dinner dishes and John had just finished showering.

" Hi. Come in."

" Craig Hunt, this is my husband Kyle."

" Pleasure," smiled Craig as he shook his hand. So this is the lucky bastard, he thought. He sized him up quickly- average height, slim but not muscular, average face (hard to judge for a guy), pretty average overall. " Come in and make yourselves at home."

John stood by as they entered, tying his ponytail. They repeated the introductions.

" So you're the resident medicine man," Kyle began amiably.

" I make no such claims in the presence of a bona fide physician," he laughed.

" I understand you've studied ayahuasca usage under the tutelage of a genuine shaman."

" Yes, as a matter of fact, I've been very fortunate in that regard. I've spent several years, all told, in the rain forest."

" It must have been a special set of circumstances, for an American to get taken under the wing of a shaman." Kyle tried not to sound sarcastic.

" Yeah. I'm still not entirely sure how it all came to be. I worked for a courier to the interior and came to know the tribe's people pretty well. The shaman was happy to tutor seeing how most of the younger members of his tribe were disinterested in his knowledge."

" A courier?" Kyle asked, genuinely curious.

" Yes. A friend flew in and out of the forest, delivering mail, medical supplies and people if necessary. Air travel was the only route available, and a lot of the missions and rudimentary hospitals relied on the couriers. There was always a little trading going on with the natives."

" How often do you go down?"

" Well, I just got back about a month ago. I'm not sure when I'll get the next opportunity. Hopefully in the winter."

John and Craig exchanged glances. So far, so good.

" You guys want anything to drink?"

" I'll take a beer," John said quickly.

" Beer?" Craig motioned to Kyle and Kelly.

" Sounds good."

" I'll get them." John got up and went to the kitchen.

" He's an interesting guy," said Kyle. " How long have you known him?"

" Since high school. We've been through a lot together."

" Kelly says you've tried this ayahuasca."

" Yes, a few weeks ago. It was very interesting, to say the least."

" You're doing it again, right?" asked Kelly. It was almost a plea. " What about Bob?"

" I'm sure he'll want to check it out. The designated baby-sitter, that is."

" Who's Bob?" asked Kyle, glancing at his wife.

" Another friend. He's offering to observe, be the straight man in case anything comes up."

" Like if anyone needs a quick ride to the hospital?" quipped Kyle.

" We don't anticipate any such need," piped in John, who emerged from the kitchen with four cold beers.

" If I had any observations, could he transcribe them for me?"

" Yeah, as long as you don't use any big words," laughed Craig.

" What sort of documentation?" asked John.

" Oh, just basic observations. Medical curiosity. I mean, I don't work for the CIA or anything." Kyle laughed at his own joke, not noticing how Craig and John exchanged another quick glance.

" That's good. We don't need any interference from the Feds," said Craig, this time glancing at Kelly, who smiled.

" OK, then we're on," said Kyle, tossing back the last of his beer. Kelly had only sipped hers, so she gave it to Kyle to finish.

" Friday it is," confirmed Craig.

" Try not to eat too much all day," John said. " Especially not dinner."

" OK. Anything else?"

" Nope. Just leave the rest to the tea."

Kyle and Kelly got up, Craig and John behind them. Craig shook Kyle's hand.   " We'll see you Friday night."

" OK. Nice to meet you. We'd better relieve our baby-sitter."

As Craig shut the door, he was greeted by another cold beer. John was quick. " You don't think Bob will mind being a medical secretary, do you?"

John laughed. " I'm sure JAMA will pay a bundle for publishing rights." He didn't realize how prophetic that statement was.

Chapter 40

Autopsy

Four days after the sudden death of his gifted assistant, Roger

Temple was still a wreck. The act of witnessing a death is traumatic

to begin with. But if the deceased is a friend and colleague, and the

cause of death may have originated by your own actions, then the

effects can be devastating. Temple was obsessed with determining

the cause of death.

He'd decided that before confronting Swenson with the factual account, he would research Stewart's death himself. There was still the remote possibility that his demise was completely unrelated to the ayahuasca. Temple's involvement may have been a bizarre coincidence. His first inquiry would have to be with the coroner who performed the autopsy. If there were no answers there, Temple would investigate further. One notable fact was that he himself had suffered no ill effects from that night's session.

Dr. Carter Smyrna had been the county coroner for eighteen years. He had taken the job during a mid-life crisis, and hadn't practiced privately for over a decade. Somehow, working with the dead appealed to him. In fact, he preferred working alone, as if any dealings with live humans rubbed him the wrong way. Thus he was in no mood to answer Temple's twenty questions.

" Coroner's office." He answered his own phones, reluctantly.

" Smyrna, please."

" This is he."

" Hi doctor. My name is Roger Temple. I'm the man who witnessed Tom Stewart's death."

" Tom Stewart?" The name sounded familiar but Smyrna wasn't about to be any more helpful than he had to.

At the other end, Temple surmised that this call was going to be more difficult than he expected. How many autopsies could this guy do in a week, anyway? This wasn't L.A. " Stewart, young Caucasian in his twenties. Preliminary report was hemorrhagic stroke."

" Oh yeah. Head damn near exploded."

Temple was shocked at the man's crass language. After all, Smyrna couldn't possibly know what relationship Temple had to the deceased. A family member would certainly not care to hear about their loved one's death in that manner.

However, Temple was encouraged by the coroner's apparent willingness to discuss the case.

" Could you determine the etiology?"

" You a lawyer?"

" No. I was Stewart's boss. We do-did-pharmacologic research."

" I don't know…This report is not official yet."

" Meaning what?"

" Meaning that I don't divulge this information to any Tom, Dick or Harry that calls me about it."

" Look Dr. Smyrna. With all due respect, I plead with you to tell me anything you've found out. You see, I'm trying to determine if Stewart's death had any relationship to the research we were doing."

" What kind of research?"

" Pharmacology."

" You mentioned that," snapped Smyrna, letting Temple know hat he wasn't born yesterday.

" It's classified."

" I see. So is my work."

Temple was discouraged. He had no clout over the coroner. If Smyrna decided he wasn't talking, that was it. He thought quickly about another approach, which luckily hit him right away.

" I'd hate to pursue this through the agency."

" What agency?" Smyrna was tiring of this conversation.

" The CIA. And before you shrug that off let me assure you that if they are called in they won't be a happy bunch."

" I've got nothing to hide."

" Nothing?"

" What are you getting at?" Smyrna growled defensively.

Temple wasn't getting at anything. He rolled the dice, assuming that everyone has something to hide, no matter how trivial. By the tone of Smyrna's voice, Temple had just rolled snake eyes.

" Oh nothing. Thank you for your time"

" Wait a minute." Smyrna paused. After all, there wasn't much reason to hide information from an autopsy that would soon be public record. " What is it you need to know?"

" What caused the hemorrhage?"

" It looked to me to be congenital. There was not a sign of organ damage due to chronic hypertension, nor was there anything in his medical records. It looked like a cerebral aneurysm, which as you know, can burst with little provocation."

An aneurysm, as Temple did know, was a ballooning of the blood vessel, often due to a congenital malformation of blood vessel walls. The weakened vessels expand, often over several years, until they finally burst. This can happen anywhere in the body, but when it does so in the aorta or cerebral vasculature, it is usually fatal.

" What about a tox scan?"

" Clear. Negative for narcotics, marijuana, cocaine, barbiturates and stimulants."

At the other end of the line came a long sigh of relief. Apparently, Stewart's death was in fact unrelated to the ayahuasca. At least, as far as this coroner was concerned.

" So, in summation, this was a death from natural causes."

" Dr. Temple, let me assure you or anyone else, nothing could have been done by you or any doctor to save this poor man." Smyrna was almost showing a little compassion. " There was a singular unusual finding, however, that may interest you."

Temple's reverie was momentarily broken.

" Oh yeah? What was that?"

" Well, may I ask what you two were doing at the time of the incident?"

Suddenly Temple was under scrutiny, and he wasn't prepared.

" What do you mean?"

" I mean, what activity were you and Stewart engaged in at the time of his stroke? You were together, weren't you?"

" Well yes, we were. But nothing unusual. We were watching TV and preparing to review our research plans for the next day." He lied through his teeth but it sounded plausible. " Why do you ask?"

" Well, his tissues were perfused with epinephrine. An adrenaline rush, if you will, as if he were suddenly frightened or highly stressed."

" Interesting," was all Temple could muster.

" Yeah. I attributed it to the shock of imminent death, the fright reaction. He probably knew he was done for, and his body reacted with a shock reaction."

" Is that common?"

" It is in situations where the cause of death is known by the victim, like armed robberies or plane crashes where the victims have time to understand their fate. Maybe Stewart had time to realize what was happening to him."

" Scary thought."

" Yep. Anything else?"

" No, thank you. I appreciate your willingness to help."

" No problem. I'll release the report findings in forty eight hours."

As Temple hung up, he was intrigued by the adrenaline rush experienced by Stewart just before his death. Perhaps ayahuasca was the culprit after all. It certainly was not a drug picked up in a post mortem screening, since few doctors know anything about it. If there was something to it, Temple needed to find out. He wasn't going to Swenson until he was positive he had all the information. The question was, where does one find out about the physiologic impact of ayahuasca ingestion?

Chapter 41

The Last Straw

Kelly awoke to find Kyle already gone to work, which was not unusual. Jason was comfortably settled in next to her, sound asleep. This was to be an uneventful day, with basic housework and possibly a short excursion to the mall in search of new shoes. The housework, of course, would depend on Jason's willingness to nap.

She slipped out of bed quietly so as not to awaken her son. She always wondered how silly that must look, not that anyone was watching. Within minutes she was sipping herbal tea and glancing at the headlines. Halfway through the tea cup she heard he familiar sounds of Jason's screaming. So much for the quiet moment to herself.

Jason quieted as soon as he latched on to her over worked breast. She was able, through weeks of practice, to maneuver through the house holding Jason while he nursed. She made it back to the kitchen, sat down, and continued with the newspaper. The phone interrupted her.

" Hello?"

" Hi honey." It was Kyle.

" Hi. What's up?"

" Nothing special. My schedule's pretty full this afternoon so I wanted to let you know not to call. What were you guys up to?"

" Not much. We're going to bathe in a few minutes."

" Oh yeah. I almost forgot. Did your mom agree to baby-sit Friday?"

" Yes. She'll swing by around seven and spend the night," Kelly said.

" What did you tell her?"

" I made up a story about a romantic night out with a champagne breakfast."

" Couldn't you come up with something she'd believe?" he joked.

" Shut up. I've always hated lying to that woman. At any rate, I told her that if she needed us, it would be easiest to beep us. That way we won't need to leave a phone number."

" What happens if she does beep us?"

" You know, I hadn't thought of that." She thought for a moment. " Well, we'll think of something."

" OK. Well, got to go. Love you."

" Love you too." She hung up. Jason, satiated with mother's milk, looked at her and smiled.

" Hi sweety. Do you want to take a bath with mommy?" He responded affirmatively with a loud belch.

Kelly stood, leaving the newspaper open on the kitchen table. It was open to the obituaries. There was one that was significant, although she didn't know it at the time:

Thomas Stewart died unexpectedly Sept. 4th. He was 24 years old.   Mr.   Stewart worked as a lab assistant in the medicinal chemistry department of Wood Labs, where he was employed for two years. He was currently working on drug screening projects for the U.S. Government under the supervision of Dr. Roger Temple.

His parents, Joseph and Helen Stewart of Grand Ledge,

Michigan and brothers Mike and Fred of Cleveland, Ohio

survive him.

Services will be held Monday, Sept. 10, at Roselawn

Cemetery, calling hours will be   Sept. 9 from 6-9 PM at

Miller's Memorial Home.

Even if she'd read the obituary, she wouldn't have known that

Stewart died indirectly from the same drug that she and her husband

would be ingesting in a few days.

Jason responded favorably to the bath idea. Kelly ran the water,

then stripped herself and Jason. Settling in to the tub, Jason began

slapping the water immediately. She brought his various floating

toys into the water and his playfulness escalated. She reached over

to shut off the water. It was almost too shallow for her to enjoy, but

it was a safe level for him as long as she held him. He looked up,

slapped water in her face, and started laughing. She slapped a little water back at him and was seized by a stomach cramp shooting through her abdominal region. She grabbed the side of the tub, thankful that the pain disappeared quickly. Hopefully, it wouldn't return.

She reached over several minutes later to carefully run some hot water to re-warm the tub. As she shut off the faucet, the pain returned, this time even more unbearable. It was like a kitchen knife slicing through her stomach. She doubled over, trying to take deep breaths. The pain increased, paralyzing her. The last thing Kelly saw before blacking out was Jason slipping out from his perch between her knees. He would be on his own for a few minutes, struggling against the hostile environment of the bathtub as his mother slumped over, unconscious from the pain.

Flopping in the water, Jason gulped several mouthfuls. Unable to get his footing, he slipped face first into the water. Kelly, still unconscious, was oblivious to the fate of her infant. Frantically,

Jason slapped at his mother's legs, coughing and crying. Finally exhausted, he slipped again, landing face first in the water. He stopped moving.

Almost simultaneously, Kelly regained consciousness. She gathered her wits, screaming upon finding Jason motionless in the water. Quickly, she grabbed his limp body and began slapping his backside for what seemed like an eternity.

" Wake up!" She screamed. She held him up to her face, trying to get a hint of his condition. As she was about to get out and attempt CPR, his body jerked, he coughed, and soon he was crying. She was never so glad to hear that cry. Wrapping them both in a towel, she made her way to the bedroom, collapsing on the bed.

" That's the last straw," she said as she brought Jason to her breast. " We're not playing around anymore."

Chapter 42

Terminated

Roger Temple approached Swenson's office confidently. With Stewart's sketches in hand, he had his story ready. He would tell the truth, and Swenson would undoubtedly support him. Or so he thought.

" Mr. Swenson, there's a Roger Temple to see you."

" Send him in." Swenson stood to greet his research scientist. " Roger, how are you doing?"

" Better, thank you."

" I'm glad you stopped by. There's something I needed to discuss with you."

" Wait," Temple said, holding up his hand. " Let me show you something very important." He held out Stewart's plant sketches.

Swenson took the sketches and looked them over, rather puzzled. " What are these?"

" The mystery ingredient we've been searching for."

Swenson studied the sketches closely. They were detailed and distinctive, yet obviously not drawn professionally. The plant depicted was not familiar to him, but that was not surprising. " Care to elaborate?"

" They were drawn by Tom Stewart." Temple said.

" When?"

" The day he died."

" So far you've explained nothing." Swenson said tersely.

" At first I was hesitant to come forward. But when I realized how potentially important these sketches were. I knew I had no choice."

" Roger, I think you've been working a few too many hours in that lab of yours."

" I know this will sound crazy, and it certainly may compromise my integrity in this research, but these sketches were drawn during an ayahuasca vision."

Swenson wasn't sure how to react. So instead, his body reacted for him. He slammed his fist on the desk.

" How dare you?" He snarled. It was obvious to Temple that this may have been a big mistake.

" Sir, you have to understand," Temple stammered.

" Oh, I understand all right. You bitched and moaned about not having enough ayahuasca for your research. We send field agents, risking their lives, some never having returned, so you can have more material, and it turns out you are stealing the shit for your own little parties!" His veins were pulsing on his forehead, beads of perspiration forming on his brow.

" Malcolm, look. It's not like that at all. What I'm trying to tell you is…."

" Don't Malcolm me!" Swenson's tirade was just beginning. " A good man died because of your little indiscretion. And I assure you, we will prosecute."

Temple was stunned. He wasn't worried so much about legal charges. There would be no proof of wrong doing, and the autopsy was officially ruled death by natural causes.

However, it was apparent that his position at Wood was probably over, along with the research he had devoted himself to for all those years. And there was a good chance that Swenson would have him black listed. He wasn't ready to give up without a fight, though. After all, his intentions had always been solid gold.

" Can I at least explain?" he pleaded.

Swenson relaxed for a minute, pausing to massage his temples. Without looking up, he waved his hand at Temple, indicating that he could indeed give his side of the story.

Temple began tentatively, owing to Swenson's volatile condition. " I knew we were pressed for time. I was afraid that if we didn't produce some human clinical trials Gibbons would pull the plug. However, I knew he was against trials involving traditional ayahuasca. He wanted isolates that at least had potentially been stripped of their hallucinogenic properties."

He was pacing now, choosing his words carefully, hoping to salvage his career. At least Swenson was listening.

" I was fairly well informed about traditional ayahuasca usage. Well enough to feel confident that I could safely ingest it myself to subjectively evaluate its effects.

" The first couple of times were very promising. I was definitely experiencing visions, and there were no ill effects. I wanted to get another opinion, and Tom was an obvious choice."

" So you threw a little party."

" Tom and I drank a little of the mixture. That's when he had the visions." Temple motioned to the plant sketches. Unfortunately, he wasn't sure the sketches could pull his ass out of the fire.

" And then he croaked," piped in Swenson.

" In a manner of speaking. He collapsed shortly thereafter. The coroner was convinced that Tom suffered from a congenital aneurysm. He would have died with or without the ayahuasca.

" I wanted to finish the project. Successfully. That was my only motivation. No one mourns Tom's death more than I do. I think he'd want us to pursue this research in his honor."

" Cut the bullshit. I don't buy the aneurysm story. All we need is to lose another test subject after knowing about Tom's demise. We're obviously barking up the wrong tree. And there will be an investigation. You have two weeks to clean out your lab. Severance will be negotiable."

With that Temple was through. His whole career was in question, let alone his current job. He walked zombie-like through the maze of corridors that led back to his lab. The worst part of it all was that Stewart's visions would be in vain. Without money, the sketches would be a hollow remnant of the most exciting research project he'd ever worked on.

* * *

As soon as Temple left his office, Swenson allowed the smile to creep onto his face. In fact, he didn't know how he'd kept a straight face throughout Temple's plea. Everything had fallen directly into his lap. Temple had essentially fired himself through his misguided research, and in the process had produced a sketch of a plant that potentially would solve their mystery. Add to that he threat of prosecution and Swenson could make it so that Temple would not be able to work for anyone else on the same project. Of course, it was a stretch that Stewart's vision and subsequent plant sketch were actually inspired by the ayahuasca. For all he knew, it was a common houseplant he remembered seeing at his aunt's house. But it was a possibility nonetheless. And Swenson would waste no time acting on it.

His first act was to phone his friends at the local newspapers. By printing a news article about the tragic death of a young researcher during an ayahuasca experiment, any further ayahuasca research would certainly be put on the back burner. That is, at least as far as any other researchers were concerned. It meant that Wood labs would have sole duties to conduct the drug research of the decade. The negative publicity would fall right into Swenson's hands. He needed to consult with his newly hired botanist to determine the meaning of Stewart's sketches. With the CIA off his back, Swenson could conduct the research the way he wanted to, and he would reap the rewards. If only he would have known about the tea, the old shaman, and their plan for him.

Chapter 43

McCloud and Gibbons

" So tell me more about this project R.O.N." McCloud stretched out in the upholstered chair opposite the window with the view of the Washington Monument. Gibbons occupied the other.

" Rejuvenation of Operational Neurons," Gibbons began as if describing the smile of his grandson. " We started the whole project in 1986 when Reagan first started to slip. We wanted a tonic, basically, that would enable his mind to stay clear enough to finish out his term without embarrassment, or worse."

" Is he really that bad?"

" It depends on what you mean by bad. If you need him to speak out against sexual harassment in the workplace to a group from B'nai Brith he'll charm you. But if NORAD detects an incoming warhead and we need a snap decision on whether to launch a counter, then I think you'll have a problem. I don't think Nancy could access her astrologer quickly enough."

McCloud laughed, but he knew it was no joke. The First Lady was known to confer with a personal astrologer on a regular basis, and it was no secret that she advised the President on many issues. Putting two and two together, the implications were somewhat unsettling.

" What did Reagan think about it?"

Gibbons responded by raising his eyebrows.

" He didn't know about it." McCloud verbalized Gibbons' gesture. " So you were gonna slip him a mickey?"

" That's about the size of it," replied Gibbons as he refilled McCloud's brandy.   " We figured what he didn't know wouldn't hurt him."

" Who did know about it?"

" The CIA, myself and Swenson. Inside the CIA, I can't be sure who was on a need to know status. I'm fairly sure Temple had caught on but we never confirmed anything with him."

" Good man?"

" He'll keep quiet. His main interest is medicinal chemistry. There wasn't much private research money out there for mind enhancement research, so he jumped on our offer." Gibbons paused to sip his brandy. Intermittent cumulus clouds created brief periods of pronounced shade outside. "It was Temple who launched the ayahuasca research. He'd done the early research years ago on the Rios Project."

" After the assassination in Brazil?"

" Still never solved, but it got the CIA's hands dirty with ayahuasca research."

McCloud stroked his beard, gazing at the panoramic view of the nation's capital. From Gibbons' sixth floor office there was a scenic view of several landmarks. It was a crisp October afternoon. The brandy was taking the edge off.

" How's the research going?"

" Not well. It's taking longer than we'd hoped, Swenson's getting impatient and there is an unconfirmed report that Temple's associate died after ingesting a small amount."

" They were sampling?" McCloud asked.

" Apparently. My guess is that Temple was circumventing the normal channels. I think he wanted to start human clinical trials before it was officially approved."

" On himself?"

" And his associate, apparently." Gibbons added.

" Do you condone this?"

Gibbons tilted his head, resulting in a cracking sound from his neck. " Do you know any decent chef who doesn't taste his own food?"

" Hardly the same. We're talking about mind blowing substances."

" You, of all people, should know better. Didn't you ingest the very same substance in the Amazon?" McCloud's travels were well documented.

" Not the same, and you know it. When a shaman makes the stuff right in front of you, takes a whopping dose himself, then hands it to you, you feel pretty confident. For all Temple knew, the tea samples he got could have been contaminated with Kimodo Dragon shit," McCloud said.

" Don't knock it until you try it." Gibbons laughed. Officially, he and McCloud were complete strangers. Off the record, they were best of friends. Gibbons was excited about the opportunity of working together with McCloud and the NSC. The conservative approach of Wood Pharmaceuticals was slowing the research at a time when it needed acceleration. Reagan's term was in its final stages and the need to maintain his image was of paramount importance to national security. McCloud's money and experience would provide the necessary shot in the arm to Project R.O.N. Of course, there was no hint that Swenson had taken a dramatically different course of action. They would find that out soon enough.

" Seriously, Temple's actions were more heroic than foolhardy, in my opinion. I think he's a man we need on our team. He's a throwback to the old guard, the chemists who ingested their research results to see first hand what their effects would be."

" I think you may be romanticizing this a little bit. You don't think he was just a tad desperate for a breakthrough?" McCloud asked.

" Maybe. It is a cutthroat industry. He may have been afraid that his time was running out." Gibbons said.

" Well, if you say he's the man, then he's the man. I hope he likes the taste of Paca."

" What's that?" Gibbons asked.

" Jungle rat. Delicious over an open fire."

" I'll tell him to bring along some hot sauce," Gibbons said.

" Getting back to that associate who died." McCloud redirected the conversation.

" Tragic," said Gibbons. " The autopsy revealed cerebral aneurysm as the cause of death."

" We need to investigate a little further. We want to be sure that it had nothing to do with ayahuasca. Cover all the bases," McCloud said.

Gibbons couldn't argue with that. Already, he felt more confident in the project with McCloud's expertise.

" One more thing." McCloud wasn't finished.

" What's that?"

" I'd like to know about John Masters," McCloud said.

" How do you know about him?" Gibbons asked, amazed.

" I'm with the NSC, remember?"

" He's a pain in my ass, that much I can tell you. He's probably the key to this whole thing, but he doesn't know it and he's been surprisingly difficult to apprehend. We finally laid off so as not to cause him too flee the country."

" Where's he now?"

" You're with the NSC, you tell me," Gibbons joked.

" Remind me to kick your ass when we get back from South America."

" He's staying with a friend in Logan, Ohio. I don't know if the friend knows what's going on, but I assume he does. We'll be able to convince Masters that it's in his best interest to help us," Gibbons said.

" I'm sure you will."

" What have you planned so far?" Gibbons asked.

" Right now we've allocated $250,000.00, transport for a party of eight to the rim of the jungle."

" Me, you, Temple," Gibbons was counting on his fingers.

" Masters, hopefully, and then room for more if needed. We'll need a guide once we get there, but money talks. I'll provide the necessary vaccination protocol."

" No one knows we're going?" Gibbons asked.

" Classified."

" Swenson? He won't take this lying down."

" By the time he finds out we'll be feeding this to the President. Oh, and one more thing. These shamans are no fools. They can sniff deceit. And they'll kill if they do. We can expect their help if we're sincere, but we have to respect their turf. Gringos are not a popular sight in the rain forest, so we'll have to be careful in order to come back

alive."

Chapter 44

Cornered

John Masters was officially declared stir crazy by Thursday. He'd been living underground at Craig's for five days without incident and he'd decided it was time to venture out. He couldn't stay cooped up forever and he figured that if whoever it was who wanted him still did, they would have gotten him by now. Something or someone had called off the dogs.

After cleaning up after himself, he dressed and gazed out the windows. Rays of sun were burning through a cloudy sky. The time had come, and he was overdue for an excursion outside the house. He didn't have a destination. He just wanted to go out there.

He stepped out onto the patio, locked the door behind him, and strutted out to the street. He taken about forty steps when he was literally hoisted into the air and scuttled to a van which had seemingly come out of nowhere. McCloud's bodyguard had physically lifted him off his feet and thrown him into a fully equipped conversion van. His head hit the miniature refrigerator as he landed.

The man sitting in the backbench seat of the van gestured toward the refrigerator. He was in his mid fifties, well groomed and from his vantagepoint on the floor of the van, John figured the man to be in better than average shape.

"Who's offering?" John asked, rubbing his head.

"Charlton McCloud. A pleasure to meet you," he said, extending his hand, smiling.

John couldn't decide whether he was in danger or not. The only other passengers in the van were the driver and bodyguard. "Sure. Got any beer?"

"Help yourself."

John opened the refrigerator and grabbed a cold beer. He then took the only unoccupied seat.

"OK. So who are you and what do you want with me?"

McCloud leaned back in his seat, folding his hands in his lap and crossing his legs. He looked John over carefully. "I mentioned my name, and in time you'll learn who I represent. For now, Bill will drive us around, Gary will make you stay put, and I'll ask you a few questions."

"Fire away," John answered nonchalantly.

"First of all, you are in no danger as long as you respect the confidentiality of this conversation. Do you feel capable of maintaining secrecy?"

"Sure, especially since I have no idea who you are or what you want."

"Gary, show our distinguished friend what will happen to his bones should he decide to divulge any of this conversation."

John turned to the front of the van. Gary, the bodyguard, was holding up a board, one inch thick and a foot square. Without blinking, he thrust his fingers through the center of the board, neatly splitting it in half. The board and splinters fell in a heap on the floor and Gary turned around without uttering a sound.

" My lips are sealed," John said.

" My name's McCloud. I'm with the National Security Coalition, NSC for short. We're here to protect you."

" Me?"

" You and all the other hapless citizens of this self destructing planet. We mean you no harm. Quite the opposite, actually."

" Are you the Feds?"

" Loosely associated with the CIA, but we work for ourselves."

" You're the ones who've been after me?" John asked.

" Not us. That's the CIA," said McCloud.

" So everyone's after me. What did I do, anyway?"

" Actually, in this instance, we are working closely with the CIA. We've been helping them with their ayahuasca research."

John's look of astonishment told McCloud he had his man. The shock value of hitting John point blank with the ayahuasca issue would erase the time consuming interrogation. McCloud knew how to cut right to the bone.

" Ayahuasca research? What's that?"

" Don't insult me. We don't have any time to waste," said McCloud.

" What do you want from me?"

" Tell me about your ayahuasca source."

" Look, I've got…"

" Bill, stop the van." Abruptly the driver moved to the shoulder of the road and parked. Turning to John, McCloud gestured toward the door.

" If the people you're in touch with in Brazil don't mean anything to you, then get out and you'll never see us again."

" OK. I'm all ears," John said.

" One of the priority projects for the NSC is to preserve the Amazon Rain Forest. Its people, its culture, and its natural resources. Our mission is simple- we're screening potential medicinal plants for future development. Our premise is that a successful plant drug will be worth far more than the land it grows in. Find a marketable drug, and the forest will be preserved. There would be more money in saving it than destroying it."

" What's that got to do with me?" asked John.

" We believe ayahuasca is a top candidate."

" For drug development?" John was astonished.

" We have two research directions- cortical enhancement and bowel purgative effects for infant colic. The research is going very well but we need more ayahuasca."

" Again, what's that got to do with me?"

" The ayahuasca you bring back from Brazil is the most active sample we've screened."

" How would you know?" John asked.

" One of our agents confiscated a small sample. It was in a jar on the kitchen table of a friend of yours, Craig Hunt," said McCloud.

John was stunned. Everything was now falling into place. It was unnerving to realize that some agency had been stalking him, all the way from Brazil to Ohio. There was no running now. He'd been made. The only question was, who are these people and what do they really want?

" Listen John, you're in no danger. We wish to hire you in an attempt to learn the secrets of the ayahuasca mixture you use. You can help us to preserve the lives and culture of the tribes men you call friends."

" How did this all trace back to me?"

" Our agents had been trying to procure as many samples of ayahuasca as they could. Not surprisingly, it was not as easy as we thought. Fortunately, one of our scouts spotted you emerging from the jungle one day with a healthy supply of ayahuasca-and from there we poked around until we learned a little about your connection. Unfortunately, we didn't know whom you were dealing with, so our project hit a brick wall. What interested us early on was that not only did your sample show the most activity, but also what little analysis we could do revealed an unusual chemical constituent. Our chemists are convinced that your blend may hold the answer."

" It's not my blend," John said.

" You know what I mean. Have you seen it prepared?" McCloud asked.

" Of course."

" Could you identify the plants?"

" Some of them."

" But not all?" pressed McCloud.

" The shaman kept a few ingredients secret, said no white man should know. I didn't pressure him. I wasn't familiar with the plants he did show me."

" We need your help to get to him."

" You don't know what you're getting into," John said.

" That's where you are wrong, Mr. Masters."

" Suppose I get you to their settlement. Then what?" asked John.

" Then with you as a mediator we explain our purpose. It's a win-win situation."

" If I refuse?"

McCloud shook his head. " The bulldozers are moving in. You can help stop them from destroying the village."

The message was powerful. John had the gut impression that McCloud was sincere. But there was something in his discourse that disturbed John. He had said something that shouldn't have come out. But what?

" Well?"

" Can I sleep on it?" John asked.

" We'll pick you up in the morning."

" Deal." The ride back to Craig's house was silent. As John stepped out of the van and watched it drive away he was left with an uneasy feeling. Rather than win-win,

he felt backed into a corner. Who was he kidding? There'd be no sleeping tonight.

Chapter 45

Secret Revealed

On the last day before eviction from his lab at Wood, Temple worked feverishly to accumulate the final bits of data from his most recent experiment. Using techniques similar to the ones Snyder and Pert used at Johns Hopkins in the 1970's to discover endorphin receptors in rat brains, Temple was hoping to discover the biochemical pathways involved in ayahuasca's effects on brain tissue. Using radioactive isotopes to trace their interaction with cerebral receptors Temple was able to map out a plausible mechanism of action for various substances found in the ayahuasca.

Viewing the photographic imagery, his task was at once simple and complex. The simple part consisted of choosing the plates which were lit up to the greatest extent. The complex part involved determining which chemicals and which receptors were involved in the reaction. Temple knew from existing research that ayahuasca was a potent inhibitor of monoamine oxidase, or MAO, an enzyme responsible for the degradation of certain neurotransmitters in the central nervous system and other parts of the body. Temple was hoping to determine in which parts of the brain the ayahuasca's MAO effect was the greatest. If he could localize its activity in a particular area of the brain, he could take his research to a higher level. Without knowing which cerebral areas were affected, it was impossible to deduce any hypothesis concerning ayahuasca's cortical enhancement properties.

The experimental design was straightforward. Temple's assistant had dissected dozens of rat brains (they were closer anatomically speaking to human brains than mice) into specific brain components. The various dissections were then combined in a laboratory blender and spun into a soupy concoction. To this was added a dilute ayahuasca mixture, as well as control solutions of tranylcypromine, a MAO inhibitor used in psychiatric medicine. Finally, a dose of radioactive labeled dopamine was added to this " cocktail".

After several hours, Temple would view the slides of brain tissue in a scintillator, which would cause those receptors locked up by dopamine to glow brightly. The idea was to determine which areas of brain function were most controlled by dopaminergic neurons. Temple wasn't convinced that dopamine was specifically involved in ayahuasca's pharmacological effects, but it was an easy amine neurotransmitter to work with in the lab, and since it was somewhat implicated in certain psychosis theories, he figured it was a good starting molecule. He knew from the monkey brain experiments that neuronal tissue growth was stimulated after exposure to ayahuasca. This experiment was designed to identify which neuronal networks were affected.

Temple began comparing the slides. First, he'd determine from the tranylcypromine slides which areas of the brain were most effused with MAO. He would then look at the ayahuasca slides and compare the relative MAO inhibition. It was a painstaking process, and the results puzzled him because of a seeming lack of any pattern. The results pointed to a heretofore unknown theory- the existence of not just the already discovered MAO A and MAO B but MAO "C", specifically in the region of the brain associated with higher emotions. Before he could even ponder his new discovery, another more shocking realization struck.

For some reason he had begun thinking about Tom Stewart. He remembered that Tom had mentioned something about skipping his dinner as advised on the fatal night, but having had a little wine and cheese instead after work. Temple collapsed in his chair, kicking out his feet and staring at the ceiling. He couldn't believe he hadn't thought of it before. Wine and cheese contain tyramine, the chemical precursor to the catecholamines like epinephrine and dopamine. Under normal conditions, the extra tyramine is metabolized and excreted. But in the presence of an inhibitor of the monoamine oxidase enzyme, tyramine is left to persist in the body and be converted to the neurotransmitters epinephrine, dopamine and 5-hydroxytryptamine. The result is a dangerous elevation in blood pressure, which can lead to a life-threatening stroke. Stewart was loaded with tyramine when he drank the tea. The neurotransmitter overload, which resulted, culminated in a meteoric rise in his blood pressure. His aneurysm was not a congenital malformation- it was the result of a fatal food-drug interaction.

Suddenly his research enthusiasm had accelerated to a frenzy. Not only had he discovered a possible mechanism for ayahuasca's action in the brain, but also he had deduced the cause of death in his associate. Tom's death had put a dark veil over his research, and although not finished mourning, Temple at least had come to realize that the ayahuasca itself was not responsible for the untimely death.

His excitement was only slightly marred by the intercom buzzing. He thought about ignoring it, but the second and third buzzes were persistent.

" Temple here." He was glancing at slides while speaking.

" Dr. Temple, this is Fred Stockton, security."

" What can I do for you, Fred?" He looked at the clock on the wall. It was four thirty.

" Dr. Swenson has informed me that you're to be out by six o'clock."

" Understood." He thought about arguing for more time, but decided not to waste his energy. His personal effects had long been packed and moved out, save for the slides he was currently working on. In all, the remainder of his tenure at Wood could easily be packed away in his worn briefcase. He had an hour and a half to sort through the three dozen or so slides. He was excited and saddened by the realization that Stewart's death could have been prevented. However, it strengthened his position that ayahuasca was still worthy of his valuable research effort. He just hoped someone out there would agree to finance his study.

MAO C. He could hardly think straight. From what he remembered from basic physiology, MAO A was found predominantly in the liver and intestines while MAO B was concentrated in brain regions responsible for regulation of blood pressure and muscular coordination. Apparently MAO C was also focused primarily in the brain, but was independent of Type B. Type C appeared to be specific for mood and emotion, and Temple theorized that it was serotonin, rather than dopamine, that was involved. Not only was serotonin targeted in some types of depression, but its role in the mechanisms of the hallucinogenic properties of LSD and psilocybin had long been theorized.

A non-specific MAO inhibitor, like tranylcypromine, would have effects on all three types of MAO. A more specific drug, like selegiline, would target only MAO B at lower doses, making it effective in the treatment of Parkinson's disease without the typical side effects. An even more specific drug, like ayahuasca, could target MAO C in the emotion center of the brain and indeed, the amygdala portion of his brain slides showed the brightest display of MAO C binding. He was on the threshold of a major discovery, but in half an hour he would be a scientist without a laboratory.

At six o'clock Temple was packed and ready to go. He stood and looked around the lab he called home for seven years. He lovingly ran his hand over the stainless steel counter top where he had labored so long. The Saturday nights, the Sunday afternoons. He wondered if he'd ever find a new home that could replace it. Soon, of course, the rain forest of Brazil would become his new lab. Stainless steel and glass would be replaced by trees and innumerable insects, his white coat by jeans and a tee shirt.

The opening of his lab security doors broke his moment of private nostalgia.

" Dr. Temple?" The security guard had just stepped inside. It was Jim Petrie. Temple knew him well.

" Coming. I'm coming. Here, it's all yours," Temple said, handing his door key card to the security official.

" Not necessary. We'll change the code. It's yours, a souvenir."

" Thanks Jim. Send my best wishes to your little woman."

" I will." He shook the scientist's hand. " Good luck, Roger. I'll miss you around here."

Temple patted him on the back and exited without looking back. He was about to embark on the greatest adventure of his life, but he already missed his old lab.

Chapter 46

Kyle's Research

Kyle progressed through his rounds very distractedly. His mind was preoccupied with the ayahuasca theories and on top of it all he'd suffered from stomach cramping, sometimes severe, all morning. He was relieved when, at 11:30, his charts were caught up and he could retreat to his office for a quick bite and a little privacy.

After pulling his salami sandwich out of the refrigerator and grabbing a Coke he set himself at his desk. Away from the watchful gaze of his well-mannered wife, Kyle gulped the sandwich like a famished street dog, washing it down with almost the entire can of cola. He punctuated the completion of his frenetic lunch with an audible belch. He laughed at his own boorish ways. Obviously, good manners were not related to a person's education or social status.

Pulling out his wallet he searched for the number Dr. Moorehead had given him for Dr. Vasquez. He dialed, and on the second ring a young sounding woman with a heavy Portuguese accent answered, identifying herself as Dr. Vasquez.

" My name is Dr. Kyle Ferguson, over at St. Luke's. I got your number from an associate, Dr. Moorehead."

" Oh yes, Dr. Moorehead. What can I do for you?"

" I had an interest in a rain forest drug, and Dr. Moorehead thought you'd be just the expert who could help me."

" Well, I'm no expert, but I did study many of the medicinal plants down there growing up. Which one are you interested in?" she asked.

" I believe it's called ayahuasca."

There was a pause on the line.

" Come again?"

" Ayahuasca? You'll have to excuse my pronunciation." Kyle figured he wasn't pronouncing it clearly enough for her to understand.

" That's what I thought you said. What in the world stimulated your interest in that drug?"

" You've heard of it?"

" Of course, but…excuse me, but you've caught me off guard."

" I'm sorry." Kyle sensed that he'd struck a nerve. " I just had some general questions."

" Sure. I happen to know a great deal about the tea. My grandfather was a shaman in the Rio Vaupes. He taught me a lot."

" Good. Hopefully I won't take too much of your time. I was wondering what it was actually used for."

To Kyle, the question seemed perfectly rational. He was therefore surprised when Dr. Vasquez responded with a hysterical laughing fit. It took a moment for her to regain her composure.

" I'm sorry. But to reduce the ancient, sacred drug to a simple 'what is it used for?' really tore my sides."

Kyle was slightly embarrassed. " I guess I've got a lot to learn about ayahuasca."

" We all do," she chuckled a last time. " It's one of the great mysteries of our existence."

" I've read the folklore concerning its supposed ability to impart telepathic powers on its users."

" Supposed, nothing. And it may be folklore to you Americans,

but to us it is as real as this telephone."

Kyle was intrigued. " So you're saying that there's something

to all that."

" Dr. Ferguson, with all due respect, the sacred vine is not

something to be taken lightly."

" I apologize if I'm not familiar with native customs. I guess

that's why I'm asking, to gain a better understanding."

" May I ask why?"

At first Kyle was hesitant to tell the story behind his inquiry.

Yet he hadn't prepared a response to her question in advance, so he

decided to shoot from the hip.

" I am pursuing a theory that ayahuasca may have a beneficial

effect of my infant, who suffers from colic."

There was another pause, giving Kyle a moment to digest the

concise manner in which he had explained himself without giving

away any of the implausible connections to shamanic rituals.

However, he was surprised by Dr. Vasquez's response.

" It's true. I've seen it in dozens of cases."

" You're serious?" Kyle asked.

" Like I said, ayahuasca is no joking matter. Used properly, it can treat infants and the infirm. Improperly, it can kill the strongest warrior."

" If it's so effective, why aren't we investigating it here?" His tone was inquisitive rather than cynical.

" It's not that simple. Let me think of an analogy. Digoxin, which comes from the foxglove plant, is effective in treating weak arrhythmic heartbeats. Physicians can safely use the tablets, refined from the plant constituents. However, the raw plant material should only be used by a knowledgeable herbalist, and even then, the plant has been known to kill. You don't use ayahuasca unless you know what you're doing, and you don't know what you're doing unless you've been a shaman's apprentice."

" Do you believe that it can facilitate telepathy?"

" The visions are real, and the message is revealed to those worthy of it. If the vine wishes its user to travel to other realms, then the user will travel. If the vine divulges knowledge unseen in the waking world, then so be it. We don't question and we don't try to investigate."

" It sounds supernatural," Kyle mused.

" It is, at least according to western paradigms of reality. The Apollo missions to the moon are supernatural events to the Putamaya."

" Do you have any theories for how it works on infant colic?"

" Depending on how you look at it, it's a combination of spiritual healing and a general purgative. Specifics, again, are not fully disclosed. If it works, it works. We don't question it."

" Well, you've been very helpful. Thank you for your time and information."

" My pleasure." She paused. " Dr. Ferguson, don't play around with the tea. Academic interest is one thing, but direct experimentation with ayahuasca is no game. If you cross the sacred boundary you may never return."

It was an ominous warning. " I understand. Thank you again."

" Good day." As she hung up, Dr. Vasquez shook her head, muttering in Portuguese. The meaning would have been lost in translation.

Kyle still had a few moments to relax before his next appointment. As he picked up the newspaper, he noted how adamant the Brazilian doctor had been concerning the dangers of ayahuasca, and how matter of fact she was about its use in colic. His scientific interest was soaring, but his fatherly instincts were causing him to sour on the idea of subjecting his son to the tea. Just then an article caught his eye which clinched his decision. It was on page four of the daily newspaper:

Bethesda, MD. A researcher employed by Wood Pharmaceuticals, under contract with the Federal Government, died yesterday, apparently after ingesting an experimental drug under investigation. The drug was identified as a rain forest herbal mixture, a known

hallucinogen called ayahuasca.

EMS crews were called to the apartment of Dr. Roger

Temple, Ph.D., the head researcher of the project. Tom

Stewart, aged twenty-eight, was pronounced dead on arrival,

apparently of a hemorrhagic stroke believed to have been

triggered by a severe drug reaction to the ayahuasca.

Dr. Temple could not be reached for comment, but a

press release issued yesterday by Malcolm Swenson, CEO of

Wood Pharmaceuticals, announced that all research on

ayahuasca was immediately suspended and Dr. Temple had

been relieved of his duties.

Swenson declined to comment on the nature of the

research. According to Brent Marshall, Ph.D., at the

National Institute of Health, ayahuasca is a potent, little

understood hallucinogenic brew found exclusively in the

Amazon rain forest. He was unable to ascertain any possible

uses for the drug, but confirmed that the fatality was quite

possibly caused by the ayahuasca ingestion.

Kyle put the newspaper down in disbelief. Not only was the content of the article alarming in light of his possible involvement with ayahuasca, but the coincidence was incredible. A few weeks ago, he'd never even heard of ayahuasca, and now he couldn't escape it. However, the combination of his conversation with Dr. Vasquez and the newspaper article clinched it- there would be no fooling around with ayahuasca. Immediately, he dialed home to update Kelly on these recent discoveries.

Chapter 47

Departure

John had to shake Craig vigorously before he could wake his

friend. It was eight thirty and the gray skies and cold drizzle didn't provide any enticement to wake up. Craig resisted as long as he could.

" What the hell…Jesus, settle down," Craig complained.

John stopped shaking him, realizing that perhaps he was being a little rough.

" Wake up, man, it's important."

" What time is it, anyway?" Craig asked.

" Eight thirty."

" Better be important," Craig said without opening his eyes.

" I'm taking off. I wanted to let you know."

Suddenly Craig sat up in bed. " What do you mean, taking off? Where you going in such a hurry?"

" Brazil." John said.

" Brazil? What about our plans?"

" Something's come up. There's no choice."

" What about Kelly and Jason?" asked Craig.

" Hopefully they're coming with me," John said.

With that Craig was completely awake. " I think I deserve a little explanation."

" I guess you're right, but I haven't much time."

" Well then, you'd better talk fast." Craig was already up, getting dressed.

" I finally got to meet the dudes who were following me."

" Oh yeah? Who were they?" Craig asked.

" They call themselves the National Security Coalition, NSC for short. They're working to save the rain forest by finding a drug to develop."

" Sounds familiar."

" Yeah, only they're convinced that ayahuasca is their miracle drug, and that I'm their best connection."

" You? How is that?"

" I really don't know, but they knew enough about me to sound convincing," John said.

" Why the rush?"

" Apparently there's been an explosive increase in development just north of Bitu's village."

" And they want you to bring Kelly and Jason?" Craig had a tinge of jealously in his voice. He was actually quite possessive over Kelly.

" Well, they don't exactly know about that part yet."

" And Kelly's agreed to go on a short notice?" Craig asked.

" Well, I haven't actually talked to her yet."

" Uh huh. And when is this trip supposed to take place?"

" In about two hours." As John spoke his voice trailed off, and his face assumed a very spaced out look to it. There was a long pause.

" Hello? Hey, space ranger… Earth to John!"

" Hold on. Something's got me confused."

" Oh yeah?" Craig said sarcastically.

John sat down on the edge of the bed. " They know all about it."

" About what?"

" About Jason's colic." John said.

" What in the hell are you talking about?" Craig asked.

" The guys from the NSC. They mentioned that ayahuasca was being researched for its cortical enhancement and purgative effects- and I believe they specifically said infant colic."

" So?"

" So how would they know about Jason?"

" How do you know they're talking about Jason?" Craig asked.

" Kind of coincidental, don't you think?"

" A lot of shit's happening that defies explanation. I'm ready for some answers," Craig said. " I'm going with you."

John looked at his friend, who by now was fully dressed and hastily packing an overnight bag.

" What?" Craig asked when he noticed that John was staring at him.

" Well, I'm not in charge, that's all."

" Look, you're saying they know about Jason. If that's true, they'll be dragging Kelly and Jason down there. And I'll be damned if I'm staying here after all we've been through," Craig said.

" Maybe you're right. Kelly's more likely to agree to this if you are a part of it."

Craig felt a surge of pride as if he was back in middle school and he heard that the pretty girl in his math class thought he was cute. As confused as he was about his feelings for Kelly, he knew one thing for sure- he wanted to be there for her during this adventure. He looked at his watch.

" Kyle's probably leaving about now."

" Aren't we a little nosy?"

" Observant," Craig corrected him. " What do I need to bring, anyway?"

" Couple days worth of clothes, hygiene stuff, like you're camping out for a weekend. We'll pick up more supplies when we reach Brazil."

" Then I guess I'm all set."

John held out his hand, which Craig shook.

" All right man. This could be the trip of a lifetime."

" Why don't I call Kelly now?" Craig offered.

" Good idea."

They went to the kitchen. John poured a few glasses of orange juice while Craig dialed.

" Hello?" Kelly sounded tired.

" Kelly? This is Craig."

" Hi. What time is it?"

" About nine. Sorry if I woke you." Craig was actually surprised. He figured most moms with little children would be up and going by nine.

" That's OK. What's up?"

" It's time." He didn't really know what to say, so he kept it brief.

" Time for what?" She asked.

" Brazil."

" I hope you're kidding."

" I wish. Something's come up, and it's apparently time for this experiment to go down."

" What's come up?" she asked.

Craig looked at John with a strained look on his face. Sensing trouble, John took the phone.

" Kelly, this is John. I know this is short notice, but this is your chance to cure Jason's colic and your own gut. I think this project is big, and I think they need your help."

" Project? Who are they?" she asked.

" There's an international consortium involved. There's too much to explain right now. But Craig and I are getting ready to go down within the next few hours."

" I don't know. Let me talk to Craig."

John handed the phone back to Craig.

" It's me," Craig said.

" What's going on?"

" John woke me a half hour ago. Apparently he was approached by these guys who are researching ayahuasca, and I guess they're onto the fact that it cures colic. They're escorting us to Brazil."

" You just found out about it?"

" Half an hour ago."

" Kyle would kill me."

" Even if it works?"

" If it works, I don't care what happens."

" So we're on?" Craig asked.

" Do we have any time to think about it?" Kelly asked.

" Five minutes."

Kelly shook her head. She couldn't imagine Kyle's rage if he came home and found her and Jason gone, off to Brazil without notice. On the other hand, she was desperate for a cure for her and

Jason's misery. If this were her chance, it would haunt her forever if she missed it. And at this point she had begun to trust Craig.

" Give me a time," she said.

" Ten o'clock." Craig looked at John, who nodded with a grin.

" What do I need?"

" We're packing for a weekend camping trip. I guess we can pick up supplies in Brazil."

" You're crazy. I'm crazy," she said.

" We're all in this together," Craig said.

" See you at ten." She hung up.

" Never in a million years," said Craig, voicing his disbelief at the strange turn of events. He slugged his orange juice. " Ahh. Now I can brush my teeth."

" Should we tell Bob?"

" He'd probably like to know," Craig said.

" He'd probably like to go!"

" Maybe he could meet us down there."

" Yeah, I'll ask McCloud." John looked out the window, expectantly awaiting the arrival of McCloud's van. He knew there was no way to prepare himself or his friends for the adventure that loomed ahead.

Chapter 48

Left Out in the Cold

Kyle's relief upon finding Kelly's van parked in their driveway soon turned to mild despair when neither his wife or son could be found anywhere. If not for the steady rain he'd expect they were out for a little stroll. Moving to the hallway, he noticed the stroller in it's usual spot, but the baby backpack was missing. At this he was getting alarmed, but thanks to his unpredictable bowel, his search would have to wait out a detour to the restroom.

" Kelly! Hey honey, I'm home! Where are you?" There was dead silence. Panicked, Kyle began racing from room to room a second time. Nothing. Out of breath, he stopped in their bedroom to rest, finding a seat on their bed. He noticed the top drawer of Kelly's dresser was open, which was unusual for her. Getting up to investigate, he decided he could not tell by looking whether anything was missing.

Returning to Jason's room, he was similarly surprised to find his top drawer open, something Kelly had yelled at Kyle for many times. At this point, Kyle suspected something strange was going on. Indeed, the diaper bag and Kelly's purse were gone. Maybe they'd gone somewhere with Kelly's mom. Although uncharacteristic, it wasn't outside the realm of possibility that Kelly had simply forgotten to call or leave a note. To that end, he dialed his mother-in-law's phone number.

" Hello?"

"Hi Adelle, it's Kyle."

" Hi sweety. What's up?"

" Is Kelly there?"

" Kelly? No, I haven't seen her. Why?" There was mild concern in her voice.

"Well, when I got home, her van was here but there's no sign of her or Jason. I thought maybe they were with you."

" No, in fact I haven't heard from her all day. I figured she'd be inside on an awful day like this, but she wasn't home. I left a few messages on the answering machine."

Kyle kicked himself- the answering machine, of course. " Maybe she's left a message there. I never thought to check."

" Please let me know."

" I will."

Anxiously, Kyle hit the play button on their answering machine and leaned on the kitchen counter to listen.

The first two messages were indeed from Kelly's mother. The third was a junk call from a local travel agency, but the fourth was Kelly. Her voice sounded strained and Kyle had to replay it twice before it sank in.

" Hi honey. It's two thirty and Jason and I are on the way to the airport. I'm sorry it came down to this. We're doing fine, and we're being escorted to Brazil for a little experiment. It all happened so suddenly there was no way to contact you. We're in good hands and we should be back in a few days. We love you, and I'm sorry."

Kyle stared at the machine in disbelief. No part of him could believe that scenario. Whatever Kelly was involved with, he had to believe that it was against her will. Although they had discussed the ayahuasca theory, he felt that it would be a group decision. The concept that Kelly had taken the situation into her own hands, grabbed their son and flown off to the rain forest with veritable strangers was beyond comprehension.

He wasn't sure what to do, but figured the police would be a good start.

He dialed.

" Logan Police."

" Hi. This is Kyle Ferguson on Maple Road. I need to report the disappearance of my wife and son."

" Disappearance?" The voice at the station seemed bored.

" That's right. When I got home from work, they weren't here, but their van was. My wife left a strange message on the answering machine."

" A strange message?"

" Yeah. Like they were being abducted and taken to the airport."

" Then I suggest you call the airport."

" You're not going to send anyone out to investigate?" Asked Kyle.

" We can't declare anyone missing until forty eight hours. Sorry."

" But that may be too late," Kyle pleaded.

" Look, Mr…"

" Ferguson."

" Mr. Ferguson. Was there any sign of foul play?"

" No, not really. But I'm not exactly an expert."

" Maybe they went to watch the planes. People do it all the time."

" Their van is still here!" Kyle shouted.

" All I can do for the time being is document your call. If there's no sign of them by, say, tomorrow night, get back to us and we'll send someone out."

Unhappy with that procedure, but with no other recourse, Kyle gave them the vital statistics. Then he grabbed for the yellow pages and the phone number for the airport. He assumed that it was Port Columbus she was referring to in her phone message.

" Port Columbus International Airport."

They answered so fast, Kyle hadn't time to think about what he was asking for.

" Yes. I need to speak to someone in security."

" May I ask what this is concerning?"

" I believe my wife and baby were abducted this afternoon and taken to the airport."

" Excuse me?" The switchboard operator had heard it all before.

Despite his near panic, Kyle realized that he probably sounded like a lunatic. " I know this sounds strange, but I have reason to believe that my wife and son were forcefully removed from our home and taken to the airport."

" I'll patch you through to Mr. Simmons."

Kyle had no idea who this was, but he'd talk to anyone at this point.

" Simmons." The voice was gruff.

" My name is Kyle Ferguson. I need to report the abduction of my wife and child. I believe they were taken to the airport this afternoon against their will."

" Which police department did you call?"

" Logan."

" We haven't heard from them," Simmons said.

" I know. They told me to call you," Kyle said angrily.

" We can't do anything at this end without the police report."

" They won't write a report for forty eight hours," Kyle said.

" Give me an ID and I'll see what I can do for you."

" You mean you'll be able to find out if they were there?"

" No promises. I'll put the word out and see what we can reel in."

" Thanks, I guess."

" No problem." As Simmons hung up, he looked at the security sheet from the official FAA log. Under the CIA/Gibbons roster were the names Ferguson, Kelly and Jason. They are in good hands, he thought.

Chapter 49

Bitu's Legacy

For Bitu, the ingestion of ayahuasca represented the perpetuation of a ritual passed down through his forebears from the initial period of the modern epoch, which according to his traditional history dates back twelve thousand years. At that point, the earth was reborn from cataclysm, and ayahuasca was given to man from the gods as a means to access the spiritual world, which prospered unaffected by earthly disasters.

According to traditions, the earth is consumed by conflagration every twelve thousand, five hundred years, in which most life is destroyed and replaced anew. In each epoch, a handful of priests and shamans are selected to carry on the traditions of past epochs. The tool selected in the modern epoch was ayahuasca, and the message Bitu received was unsettling.

Apparently, the end of the modern epoch was rapidly approaching. In fact, the vine told Bitu that he was the last shaman in the long procession of the modern period. He was to witness the next cataclysm. In the meantime, he was implored to create a global need to stop the destruction of the rain forest in order to preserve the precious ayahuasca. He was charged with the task of exposing as many individuals as possible to the sacred tea. And he needed a great deal of help to accomplish that task.

The chosen strategy was to enlist the help of the Americans, who were interested in developing a drug that could, if successful, channel a great deal of capital back to the rain forest. The vine warned him that some of the men involved had less than admirable motives. As he knew the time was rapidly approaching that would bring these men to his sacred lands, he needed to determine his allies.

The village was relatively quiet as he emerged from his hut several hours after sunset. There were numerous power spots in close proximity to the village, each with its own energy level. Bitu chose a large outcropping of rock said to have been deposited following the last epoch. To the villagers, the rock simply looked like it didn't belong. To a geologist, a rock weighing several tons, comprised of a type of granite that was not found anywhere else in the vicinity, was a scientific anomaly. To Bitu, it was a place of power.

In his satchel was a gourd full of ayahuasca, a cup fashioned from bone to drink the tea out of, and several sacred necklaces. The rock was only a five-minute walk from his village, yet he knew he would be undisturbed there. Although the ayahuasca sessions were usually done in groups, it was not unusual for the shaman to partake in solo sessions. Especially in a situation such as this where he was seeking important information on the impending confrontation with the white men.

The rock was oblong, about sixty feet long, twenty feet wide and twenty-five feet tall. It was no easy task to ascend to the top, but Bitu knew where the footfalls were and easily climbed to the peak like a gymnast. In daylight at the peak he was afforded a breathtaking view of the valley, and off to the north the sun would shine off the mountains near the village of many of his relatives. At night, he could just barely make out the outline of the mountain peaks against the darkened sky.

Methodically, he unpacked his gear. After chanting for several minutes, he transferred some of the ayahuasca from the gourd to one of the small cups and drank it. Despite the overwhelmingly bitter taste, Bitu was so accustomed to it that his facial expression remained unchanged. The flat peak of the rock was bordered by a semicircle of various boulders ranging in size from a foot to several yards across. In anticipation of his forthcoming rendezvous with the soul of the vine, he leaned back onto one of the rocks and waited.

The practice of ayahuasca ingestion predates written history. It is undoubtedly the most widely used and little understood hallucinogen in the world, and one of the few considered to be a cure-all for any ailment, in any patient. The mixture Bitu uses was passed to him during his apprenticeship with Kaligo, the elder shaman of Bitu's tribe who passed away several decades ago. Kaligo showed Bitu the " Secret Garden" where all the sacred plants for the ayahuasca were cultivated and had been for centuries. Banisteriopsis Caapi, the large woody vine comprising the main ingredient, grew in various locales throughout the Amazon basin. However, Bitu learned through Kaligo's teachings that when grown in proximity of the other sacred plants used in the mixture, the banisteriopsis acquired unusual properties. It was a trick of botany, not yet discovered by modern scientists, let alone understood. For

Bitu and his tribe, it meant having access to a powerful version of the mysterious tea. After the short wait, Bitu's visions began.

To the uninitiated, ayahuasca intoxication is anything but structured. For most of the untutored, it is a three dimensional nightmare in Sensurround. For those able to control it, the tea session is a cornucopia of visions relating past, present and future events. There is usually some form of travel involved, both in time and space. A masterful shaman like Bitu will be in complete control of the experience and can serve as a guide to new initiates.

Bitu knew of the white men who were coming from the north. Some of them he recognized, others he did not. Although their goals were similar, their motives were worlds apart. They were not all the enemy.

Bitu saw the young mother and baby. Innocents, yet they held the key to the whole mission. He saw the colonel and the entrepreneur, old friends whose paths took different turns but crossed every so often for missions such as this. Then there was his apprentice John, sincere but naïve, his friend who would return to his homeland a new man. Bitu's visions then revealed two others, whose motives were unclear. The business executive and the botanist. The vine warned of these men, but Bitu didn't know why. Often the vine never explained.

As Bitu's physical self reclined on the anomalous boulder, nestled in the Amazon water shed, his soul took to flight. He soared throughout the basin. He saw no other person and realized at that moment that he was the only human. And he realized that that moment was just after the destruction of the world, the end of the last epoch. He noted that the rain forest never changed. He knew the end of the current epoch was rapidly approaching, though he didn't know exactly when. He knew the forest would remain, unchanged. He wondered what the people would be like. That would be the subject for a future journey. There was only so much one could accomplish in a single session.

Bitu realized it was time to return. It could be done instantaneously, but he preferred the scenic route. Opening his eyes, he detected the slight brightening in the eastern sky. His session had lasted all night. He had learned that within days his cherished lands would be the battleground for his last war. He wondered how the invaders from the north would be able to handle the realization that

their world would soon come to a startling halt.

Chapter 50

Journey

Kelly gazed out the window of the Cessna as it flew over the canopy of the eastern basin. It was, she felt, the most beautiful scenery she'd ever seen. The velvet green was punctuated by meandering rivers and breathtaking waterfalls and occasionally dotted by small, primitive villages. Gazing in the other direction, toward the north, she saw what appeared to be a large smog cloud hovering menacingly over the forest.

"What's that?" she asked of anyone who could answer. The plane was set up with a very open cabin, and she could easily talk with any of the other passengers. McCloud and Temple were in the back seats, John in the middle, and Craig was across from her and Jason. All were staring out the windows.

"Destruction on a grand scale," came the reply, courtesy of McCloud from the back row.

"What are they doing?"

"Clearing the trees. Probably for a new collecting station."

"Collecting? What are they collecting?"

"Oil. Lots of men, lots of oil. Trees are a nuisance."

"Says who?"

McCloud started to laugh. It was the laugh of a learned, paternal man. So far, what she'd seen of McCloud was impressive. It was obvious that the man had money. But what was not so obvious at first, but what was becoming apparent, was that McCloud was an intelligent, compassionate man. In fact, his first act upon meeting Kelly and Jason was a request to hold the infant, and he did so with the gentleness of a grandfather. Yet he was not really old, probably not even fifty. Within minutes of meeting him, it was clear that he was the type of man that you wanted to know everything about, but never would. She could think of one word – charisma.

"Says the developers," he said. "They have a need to control nature and they don't consider the consequences."

"What companies are down there?"

"All of them." He pointed to the pollution that caught Kelly's eye first. "That construction over there is probably Yukon Oil. They've been particularly aggressive this year."

"What gives them the right?"

"Money."

"Can't anyone stop them?" Kelly knew she must have sounded naïve, but she couldn't fathom the idea that big business could just slash and burn the forest that way.

"We're going to try." McCloud said it so matter of factly that it sounded like it was already a done deal.

"What makes the drug development scheme different from oil extraction?"

"Not all big business is destructive," said John, speaking up for the first time.

"What if the oil companies destroy it all before we can develop the drug?" She at least had caught on to that line of thinking.

"It will be a struggle, for sure. That's why we gave you such short notice," McCloud said.

"Short notice? How about no notice?"

"See? We mean business."

Kelly caught Temple's eye in the cabin mirror. "So you're the drug expert here?"

"At your service."

"I take it you are a firm believer in this scheme?"

Temple had to laugh. "Yes, I am. As long as there's money in it for me."

"Some philanthropist you are!" Soon everyone was laughing, even Craig.

Up to that point, Craig had been rather sullen. There was so much commotion that Kelly hadn't had the chance to talk with him.

"You don't look so hot. Does flying bother you?" She asked.

"No. Not really. I'm just thinking about how my boss is gonna rip out my intestines and hang me from the rafters with them when I get back."

"Didn't you tell them you were leaving?" asked John.

"Yeah, but all I told them was family emergency. They wanted details."

"Why? I mean, what's the difference?" Kelly asked.

"Because Monday was an important court date, and I was the lead attorney. They'll have to scramble to fill in if they can't postpone the trial."

"As least you spoke to them. All I did was leave a message."

"Do you think Kyle will understand?"

"I don't know. I'm trying not to think about it."

"If either of you need to relocate with new identities, just give me the word," McCloud said. If not for his smile, Kelly and Craig would have taken him seriously. Actually, he probably did have the capability of doing that sort of thing.

"No thanks. I'll take my chances," said Kelly.

"Yeah, me too," said Craig. "Although, if you could write me a note to turn in that confirms my family emergency, I'll accept that."

"Sure. What do you want? Death verification? Accident victim?"

"Let me think about it." Craig laughed.

Kelly decided to turn her attention back to Temple. "How does this work? I mean, what do we do, sit around and drink while you sit there in your white coat and take notes on a clipboard?"

Temple looked at McCloud as if to say 'where did she come from?' McCloud just shook his head.

"Do you always stereotype people?"

"Sorry. I didn't mean anything by that."

"No problem. But actually, yes, that's fairly accurate. I will observe your reactions to the tea, and if they are favorable, then we'll find out the ingredients and research it further back in the lab."

"If they are favorable?" Craig asked.

"We're maintaining a little skepticism in the name of good science."

"How many trials do you think it will take?" Craig asked.

"From what I've been led to believe, one."

"How will we determine success?"

"We'll go by your subjective responses," Temple said.

Kelly thought about that for a minute. "So it's up to me and Jason."

"Yes it is. Presumably, his colic will disappear with the first dose."

Kelly looked down at her baby. Miraculously, he'd slept most of the trip. As if in response to her gaze, he stretched his arms, yawned, looked up at her, and went back to sleep.

"How do they know how much to give?"

"They've been doing this for hundreds, maybe thousands of years," said John.

"I guess," she said. "Are you guys going to drink it too?"

"I am," said John. He looked at Craig.

"Me too, if I'm invited."

"Mr. McCloud?" she asked.

"Charlton, please."

"OK, Charlton, will you be drinking the tea with us?"

"I think I'll leave that up to the shaman."

"What's he like, anyway?" she asked John.

"He's older, about sixty or seventy and very quiet. You'll probably think he's scary at first, until you get to know him."

Kelly returned her gaze out the window. She tried to imagine what a genuine medicine man of the Amazon would be like. Temple had just kidded her about stereotyping people, but she found herself doing it anyway. Painted face, beaded necklace with jaguar teeth, grass skirt. She found herself becoming very anxious for the proceedings to begin. Just then, the yellow cabin light began blinking. They were about to descend into the primeval rain forest, her first meeting with the shaman just hours away. Or was it her first meeting?

Chapter 51

Preston's Folly

For the first time in his illustrious career, Marty Preston would feel foolish, trampling with his guide through the forest with a sketch of an unknown plant he needed to find. Swenson had given him the usual allowance necessary to perform the task and make a comfortable profit, but the sizable bonus upon finding the plant was Preston's real motivation. And it was sizable enough to make

Preston not so concerned about what he would look like trampling through the woods with a sketch of an unknown plant in his hand.

Based upon Swenson's descriptions of the plant as an ingredient in ayahuasca, Preston's guide decided they should concentrate their efforts in the regions known for their banisteriopsis population. Otherwise, his search would be insurmountable. There were several specific locations that he knew supported large numbers of banisteriopsis vines. With his guide he headed for the closest.

Much of the travel is by boat and Preston had made several connections over the years. With enough persistence and money one can procure a suitable guide into almost any region of the rain forest. Preston had plenty of both.

The son of a prominent Boston physician, Preston graduated from high school with many dreams but no real plan. He was unsure about college, but his father had secured his admission into Harvard behind his back. Once on campus, he was still no closer to deciding on a career plan. Needing a little spending money, the young freshman applied for a job watering plants at the Harvard Botanical Museum. He never looked back.

Harvard's Botanical Museum has been one of the world's leading institutions for the study of exotic plants. Preston was hooked, feeling for the first time in his life as though he found something that truly interested him. He began undergraduate studies in biology and botany and within seven years had earned his doctorate. All the while he worked at the museum.

During his many field trips to the Amazon, he was amazed by the economical potential of the rain forest plants. He found himself the target of many offers, ranging from drug companies to florists. Apparently, there was a tremendous demand for exotic plants, and as long as it was legal Preston was happy to oblige- for a price. His reputation grew as a reliable and efficient plant hunter, and soon he was able to make a comfortable living. His reverence for the rain forest, however, never wavered. His plant collections were conducted with much care not to disturb the ecology. And no matter what plant was requested, he would always collect an extra specimen for the museum. Harvard Botanical was like a zoo that perpetuated endangered species, and Preston was one of the top curators.

This particular mission was unusual in that his target plant was basically an unknown. The sketch given to him by Malcolm Swenson was fairly detailed, but with half a million species underfoot it seemed impossible. He and Swenson had agreed on the terms of Preston's mission – two weeks of searching, which would guarantee Preston a stipend of ten thousand dollars. If he found the plant, he would expect an additional twenty five thousand dollars. Preston knew one thing for sure. He would not find the plant by bumbling through the forest. He would need someone to show him the way, someone that knew the territory. His first stop was the Catalina Hotel in Belmopan, Belize, to meet with his old friend Carlos Ventosa. Carlos could quickly and safely guide Preston to several villages in the basin where the botanist could contact several shamans. Preston was also loaded with various gratuities with which to bribe his contacts. It never hurts to make friends.

Preston had picked up Ventosa in the lobby of the Catalina. They sat at the bar for a couple of beers while they outlined their itinerary mapped out on a tattered hand drawn rendition of the target region, courtesy of a cocktail napkin. There were few patrons in the hotel bar, the ceiling fans lazily spinning, off balance, above their heads. The heat of the mid afternoon was stifling and Preston was anxious to head for the forest.

Ventosa had a car, and within forty-five minutes they reached a checkpoint. There they could rendezvous with an emaciated, elderly native who had a boat waiting. It was no frills travel and Preston enjoyed every minute of it.

Winding down the tributary, the sun would occasionally burn through an opening in the trees and would quickly scorch unprotected skin. After a few hours, the boat landed on a bank of the river, where the boatman bade them farewell.

Ventosa was normally a very jovial person, and once they hit landfall his personality came through.

"Let me see again what we are looking for."

Preston showed him a copy of the sketch.

"Yage?" He asked, referring to the native word for ayahuasca.

"That's what we believe," said Preston swatting a mosquito.

"That's all you have?" asked Ventosa, holding up the sketch.

"Yes. That's it," he said, enunciating clearly.

Ventosa's laughter was contagious. Preston laughed, realizing that it was OK for him to feel foolish. After all, here they were, two insignificant men amidst the majesty of the primeval rain forest, searching for a singular plant among countless others.

"I swear, I think even the animals are laughing," Ventosa jeered.

As they walked, machetes in hand, Preston kept his eyes moving, both for the predators and to gaze at the foliage. For a botanist it was true heaven. He wished he had endless time to examine the lush surroundings. Time, however, was a luxury he did not have.

"How long?"

Ventosa scratched his head. "Oh, another hour. We'll pass the…"

He stopped dead in his tracks. Just ahead on the trail, the tail of a large snake disappeared into the brush. Ventosa hadn't time to identify it.

"What is it?" asked Preston nervously.

"Snake."

"Oh," he said, hiding his fear. He hated snakes.

Ventosa ventured forward, Preston staying put. He motioned for Preston to follow, which the botanist did reluctantly.

"You no like snakes?" Ventosa asked.

"I can live without them."

"Me too. Until I hungry." He laughed. They walked without talking for another thirty minutes, coming to a clearing. Ventosa bent down, motioning for Preston to do the same. Marty duck-walked up to Ventosa, peering over the brush. In the distance was a village, but it was too far to see details.

"We'll go talk to them. I'm sure they'll be helpful," said Ventosa as he stood. Both men turned around and were immediately greeted by the tips of spearheads in their throats. Two warriors glared at them from the other end of the spears.

Chapter 52

Arrival

The entourage transferred from McCloud's plane to Roja's

plane directly on the tarmac. The heat so stifled Kelly that she had

difficulty breathing. She was careful to keep Jason covered from head to toe as he was still too young for sunscreen. The tropical sun overhead scorched everything it touched. Kelly's sneakers felt like they were melting with each step on the concrete.

Roja's plane was much less comfortable than McCloud's. The seats were crammed into a smaller area to allow for a limited cargo area, and most were tattered. Kelly watched from the window as Rojas, John and McCloud held a meeting on the tarmac. After a rather animated discussion, they reached some sort of agreement. Rojas walked around the plane as McCloud and John came on board.

"Anything wrong?" Craig asked John.

"No, not really. Carlton had packed a crate of food supplies, but Rojas is a little worried about weight, so we agreed to leave it behind."

"How much could it have weighed?"

"525 pounds."

"Shit, that's a lot of munchies."

"So, what will we eat?" asked Kelly. That was the one thing she hadn't even thought about.

"Not to worry. We brought two smaller crates, plus there is plenty of food in the forest."

"Yeah, I've heard about that food."

"Don't knock it until you've tried it."

"If it's so good, why did you bring twice your weight in rations?" she joked.

"I beg your pardon. Three times my weight!"

The engines quickly drowned their combined laughter out as Rojas readied the plane to taxi.

Kelly was continuously surprised, but pleased, at the lighthearted mood of this diverse group. If they were faking for her benefit they were terrific actors. The only person who seemed nervous was Craig.

"It'll work out," she said, tapping his knee. They were crammed so tightly it was hard to keep her hands in her own lap.

"I know. I need to stop worrying about it," Craig said, referring to his court date. "Maybe I'll start a new career as a shaman after this adventure."

The view from Rojas' plane was even more spectacular than McCloud's. With no other planes in the airspace, Rojas could lazily fly close to the canopy. Kelly was thankful for a window seat.

"It's amazing."

"Gives a whole new meaning to wooded lot," said Craig, reading her mind.

"Wait until you get down there. It's a whole new world," said John.

The flight took a little over an hour. Jason had woken up, and as usual, was crying. In the cramped quarters, it was hard for Kelly to nurse him. Craig moved over a few inches, which made it almost comfortable for Jason.

"Going down," shouted Rojas from the cockpit. With that, the plane took a dive that seemed exaggerated. At that point Kelly couldn't make out anything that remotely resembled an airstrip.

"What do we do, land on top of the trees?"

"There's a small airstrip about five miles from the village."

"Five miles?" she asked, imagining a rather difficult walk through dense forest.

"Yeah. Give or take a mile. We'll load the supplies onto a boat."

"Can I assume we go with the supplies?"

"Well, most of us. You and Jason will have to walk," Rojas joked.

"Watch out, I brought my lawyer along," she said, nodding to Craig.

"Jungle law doesn't recognize his degree."

Rojas began a sweeping turn in preparation for landing. The plane was practically sideways, making it difficult for Kelly to hold on to Jason. As the airstrip came into view, Kelly was surprised to see that there was no concrete or blacktop. The landing strip was a long dirt path, and there were only a few outbuildings scattered about. The landing was rather bumpy and the plane kicked up a small cloud of dust as it came to a stop near the end of the runway. A small group of natives approached the small plane as Rojas nudged the door open. Without cutting the engines, he departed the plane and began talking to the small group.

John saw someone he recognized, and exited as well.

"We're here," said McCloud as he peaked around the retaining wall of the cockpit. He had spent the flight acting as copilot.

"Is it OK to depart?" Craig asked. "It's been a long flight."

"Sure. Follow me."

One by one, the passengers departed. Kelly had to perform a balancing act with Jason, as the steps were a bit unstable. Immediately, they headed for one of the shacks at the edge of the runway, seeking protection from the relentless sun. It was past six o'clock by Kelly's watch, but it was still hot, in the eighties at least. Kelly watched as John joked with the arrival party. They were all obviously well acquainted. Finally, he and McCloud joined the rest under the roof of the shack.

"The boat is waiting. They'll start loading right away," said John.

"They load for us?" Kelly asked.

"Not for free," added McCloud.

She watched as six young men packed their belongings onto a pushcart and headed toward the wooded area to the right of the runway. They seemed unaffected by the stifling heat. Kelly guessed that the river was just beyond the trees.

Rojas walked over to the group. He shook hands with McCloud, who handed him an envelope, and hugged John. "Enjoy your stay. I see you in three days."

They watched as he ran to his plane, engine still running, and he quickly took off. The jungle became wonderfully quiet as the plane faded out of sight and sound.

"Come on. We want to travel in daylight." John ushered them to a small path that led to the wooded riverbank. Awaiting them was a small armada. The larger of the flat hulled boats carried their supplies, while four smaller craft were waiting for live transport. There was nothing comfortable about it.

After they had situated themselves, the boatmen pushed off and the descent toward the village commenced. It would take nearly an hour to reach their destination. Along the way the travelers were treated to a glimpse of one of the few unspoiled wilderness areas left in the world. The lazy, winding river provided a peaceful journey. Although they knew otherwise, it was hard to imagine the dangers that lurked there.

"Village up ahead," the boatman in Kelly's boat yelled as he pointed up to the left. With that, everyone secured his or her belongings and prepared to beach the boats. There were half a dozen teenage boys waiting to receive the armada.

John was the first on land, and he immediately approached one of the men. It was Yaru, the chief's son. They embraced, and after talking a few moments, Yaru pointed off toward the village. In the distance, an older man was making his way toward the group.

Craig helped Kelly and Jason off the boat and their supplies were neatly stacked on shore as the boatman headed back.

"Well, let's go see about our hotel room," Craig said, his arm on Kelly's back. He noticed she was intently staring at the old man, now close enough to see his face.

"I wonder who he is?" Craig asked.

Kelly would have answered, had she been able to speak. There, thirty feet away and smiling at her broadly, was the shaman who had visited her in her dreams so many nights ago.

Chapter 53

Interrogation

Kyle had canceled all of his morning appointments. He was sitting across the desk from a Lt. Peters of the Logan Police Department. Peters was a short, stocky man whose added weight and thinning hair added ten years to his appearance. Kyle was enjoying a cup of coffee, not having slept at all for almost two days. Peters was cursing the typewriter as he tried to fill out the missing persons report.

After telling the story for the twelfth time, Kyle was ready to go.
Peters looked over the report and nodded his head in satisfaction.
He pulled it from the typewriter and leaned back in his chair.
Missing persons in Logan County were usually drunken fishermen
who'd passed out in the woods somewhere. A mother and her infant
were in a different league.

"Now what?" asked an impatient Kyle.

"We'll put out and APB, and we'll need to send a detective over
to your house."

"What about the airport?"

"Yeah, we'll also send a man out there."

"Is that it?" Kyle asked.

"What do you mean?"

"I don't know. It doesn't seem like it's enough."

"I know it's not an easy time. But believe me, your wife and kid
out there, we'll find 'em. It's our priority case right now."

Kyle stood and shook Peter's hand. "Thank you. Please call as soon as you hear."

"Ten Four. By the way, can you leave us a key or leave the door unlocked so we can poke around?"

"Sure."

Pointing to Kyle's pager, Peters asked if Kyle wanted them to page him.

"That would be great. I'm not home a whole lot."

Kyle was only slightly relieved as he headed home. Although the police were doing everything they could, Kyle knew that the answer would come from the airport. He was also bothered by the fact that he knew their disappearance had something to do with ayahuasca, but he didn't want to bring that issue into the forefront.

He didn't think that Kelly had simply left him. He knew she was disappointed in his long work schedule, but the time they spent together was quality time. And she knew that it wouldn't be long before his schedule eased up a little. No, she didn't leave permanently. By the same token, she had left, and possibly on her own free will. Which explained his periodic feelings of anger. He just couldn't get himself to believe that she would have endangered their son without his consent.

As he pulled into his driveway, he was surprised by the presence of a detective from the Logan Police Department. He was busily inspecting the outside perimeter of the house. He approached Kyle's car with his badge out reflecting in the afternoon sun.

"Detective Tyra. Mind of I look around?"

"Go right ahead," said Kyle as he got out of his car. "Mind if I tag along?"

"No. Quite all right." Tyra turned to look at Kyle. "Any ideas?"

"No. It's a total mystery."

"Uh-huh." The detective sounded sarcastic. It seemed as if he didn't believe Kyle, but Kyle decided not to jump to conclusions. "Doesn't seem to be any sign of trouble."

"No. But isn't it odd that her car is still here?"

"That it is. Mind if we go inside?"

Kyle gestured to the front door and followed Tyra into the family room.

"How would you describe your relationship with your wife, Mr. Ferguson?"

"Dr. Ferguson."

"That's right. My apologies."

"It's OK. We have a great marriage, anyway. Couldn't be happier. Why, am I your chief suspect?"

"Spouse always is."

Kyle suddenly realized that the detective was probably serious. It hadn't occurred to him until then that he would be considered responsible for the disappearance of Kelly and Jason. That, combined with Kelly's involvement with possible drug experimentation, gave him second thoughts about the police in the first place.

Tyra interrupted his daydreaming. "Mind if we talk?" he asked.

"Huh? Oh, sure." Kyle led him to the kitchen. "Want something to drink?"

"No thanks. Go ahead." He had pulled out his notebook and began writing.

"Now, exactly when did you last see your family?"

"Yesterday morning. I left for work at seven thirty."

"They were sleeping?"

"Yeah. Jason's colicky, he still sleeps with us."

"Sounds like a good time."

"Tell me about it."

"When did you last speak with your wife?"

"That would have been the night before. I was on rounds all day, and as far as I know she didn't try to reach me."

"Would she phone or page you?"

"Both."

"In case of emergency, would you assume that she would page you?"

"Probably."

"Your pager works OK?"

"Yeah, shit. I got paged every ten minutes it seemed."

"Have you exhausted all possibilities, friends for family?"

"You mean visiting, without telling me, for two days?" Kyle sneered.

"Just covering the bases."

"No. No one has seen them."

"You say she left a phone message?"

"Yeah. Let me replay that for you."

They listened to the message. Kelly sounded calm and collected.

"Sounds OK, but you never know. With a gun to your head, it's amazing what you can do."

"Please don't say that."

"Sorry. Anyway, I'll take this to the lab, see what they can find out."

"It's all yours."

"Why would she be going to Brazil for an experiment? Any ideas?"

"Got me."

Tyra stared piercingly at Kyle, who was forced to look away.

"Sounded matter of fact, like she was planning this for while."

"What are you implying?" asked Kyle defensively.

"I don't know. It just sounded like she didn't think you'd be surprised."

"Believe me, I was surprised."

"What type of experiment do you think she may have been referring to?"

"Look, I don't have any idea what she was talking about."

Tyra stood and gazed out the window absentmindedly. "Well, if any ideas pop up please let me know." He gave Kyle his card.

"What now?"

"We'll analyze the tape and then check with the airport. Oh, do you mind if I look around real quick?"

"Go ahead."

Tyra breezed through the house. It didn't seem to Kyle that he was taking anything in, but perhaps the powers of observation for a seasoned detective are beyond Kyle's comprehension. When he finished, he shook Kyle's hand at the front door.

"OK, I'll get on it. Don't worry, we'll get to the bottom of this, one way or another."

"Thanks, let me know." Kyle leaned on the door after it shut. "Son of a bitch." He muttered to himself.

Chapter 54

Day of Judgement

Kelly had not the time or fortitude to reconcile in her mind the confusion and anxiety generated within her psyche at the sight of Bitu, smiling benevolently at her from the shore of the quiet Amazon river tributary. The excursion to the rain forest would prove to be a whirlwind of activity, with much to do in a very short time.

The living arrangements were less than comfortable for her, not physically but rather socially as she and Jason were grouped with both Craig and John. It was a one-room hut with no privacy, and the logistics were somewhat tricky. Fortunately, she had little time to dwell on it.

They planned to spend two nights in the village, the first night being earmarked for the ayahuasca session. That served two purposes. Firstly, there would be no chance to worry about it. Like the doctor who injects a hypodermic syringe without warning, the less preparation the better. Secondly, the session would likely prove tiring, giving the troop an extra night to recover. Kelly was excited and anxious to get on with it.

McCloud, John, Temple and Bitu held a meeting shortly after their arrival. This motley group set about a game plan by which the ayahuasca would be administered and the results documented. It was agreed that Temple and McCloud would abstain. Bitu and Jason would ingest with Kelly, John and Craig, if Craig were interested. The dose for Jason would be minuscule. As they gathered in a clearing near Bitu's hut, the unmistakable drone of Jason's crying broke the monotonously quiet jungle backdrop.

"That kid does cry a lot," McCloud noted.

"It will end soon," said Bitu, cryptically.

"You want me to bring them at sundown?" John asked.

"Yes, that will be fine." Bitu's English was remarkably fluent at times.

"If you don't mind, I'd like to set up my station right away," said Temple.

"Station?" asked John.

"You know, supplies. Aside from recording the sessions, I'll try to monitor blood pressure, temperature, basically document the whole event."

"What do you mean record?" asked Bitu.

"Document is what I meant. No pictures."

Bitu had made it clear he wanted no photos. Temple wasn't going to argue with him.

"Feel free to set up as you wish."

Meanwhile, Craig and Kelly and Jason were preparing. Craig had gone to the riverbank to wash and change clothes, giving Kelly the privacy of the hut. Jason, of course, had been crying non-stop.

"I still don't know what to believe," said Kelly.

"What do you mean?"

"I swear I saw that man."

Craig was silent.

"Am I crazy?" she pleaded.

"No, I'm afraid not."

"So you believe all the hocus pocus?"

"Why not? There's a lot of shit I believe, even if I don't understand it," Craig said.

"That's what scares me."

"What do you mean?"

"I kind of believe it too. Which means that this shaman really did travel across space and time to diagnose my illness."

"You described an interesting bedside manner too."

"Yeah. I hope Kyle doesn't have the similar procedure of straddling his patients in bed." They laughed. Humor helped conceal their apprehension. Just then John entered.

"Ready?"

"I guess," said Kelly.

"You sound hesitant."

"No. Just exhausted."

"This is nothing like you'll feel tomorrow."

"Just let me sleep."

"Deal. They're all ready for you."

Craig grabbed Kelly's hand and they followed John to their date with the shaman.

Although the members of Bitu's tribe had been very hospitable, there was no sign of them by nightfall. John explained that Bitu had made them stay out of sight. Kelly was relieved, when upon arriving at the designated clearing there were no unfamiliar faces. Bitu was, as usual, smiling. A set of crudely made wooden benches was arranged in a semicircle around a campfire. Temple was outside the circle at a makeshift table. He was already taking notes.

Bitu motioned for them to sit and he promptly began chanting unintelligibly. Nightfall came fast. The campfire was extremely smoky, and McCloud explained that they had thrown a natural insect repelling bark into the fire to discourage mosquitoes. So far it was working. Methodically, Bitu began removing several small cups from his leather satchel. He then poured a small amount of ayahuasca into each cup and handed one to Craig, John and Kelly. He then produced a small, ornate device and poured a small amount of the tea into it. He motioned for the adults to drink the tea.

John heartily drank his, then Craig, who once again shuddered from the aftertaste as he'd done the first time. Finally, Kelly drank hers. It was all she could do to fight vomiting. She couldn't imagine what Jason's response would be. It was time to find out.

Bitu gently beckoned for Kelly to bring over her baby. Jason was crying, of course, and Bitu was remarkably at ease with him. As the shaman made eye contact with Jason he stopped crying. Carefully positioning the device over Jason's mouth, he poured what couldn't have been more than a few milliliters into the infant's mouth. Temple was right there taking notes.

McCloud stared transfixed at the proceedings. He'd witnessed many similar healings, but none whose outcome could be so significant. He watched as Kelly and Craig exchanged glances, first with each other, then with John. They were waiting. And waiting.

Kelly would later learn that the tea preparation was extremely weak. The purgative dose is much less than the vision-inducing dose, Bitu would explain later. Therefore, there was little in the way of full blown hallucinations. Instead, she felt energized, invigorated with an overall feeling of euphoria. She felt better than she had in a long time.

Bitu held Jason in his arms for over two hours, singing softly. Jason had a look of total contentment on his face. He also had stopped crying.

Temple gestured with his stethoscope to McCloud. McCloud nodded indicating it would be OK to examine the baby. In fact, as Temple approached them, Bitu changed positions to allow for easier examination. Temple checked Jason's pulse, temperature and general physical status. When finished, Bitu handed Jason to Kelly.

"What now?" she asked.

"We sleep. First, check his diaper." It seemed incongruous to Kelly for a primitive shaman to use a modern term like "diaper".

Kelly positioned Jason on the bench. She was not prepared for what awaited her inside Jason's diaper. All was silent until McCloud broke the silence, staring at the infant's soiled Huggie.

"Holy shit!"

Chapter 55

Hostages

The scene reminded Preston of a B Movie, where the hero is captured by headhunters, then tied to a post in front of a huge pot of boiling water to view the venue of his demise. There he was, along with Ventosa, bound to a tree, guarded over by a pair of native warriors. They were on the outskirts of the village, making identification of the tribe impossible. It had been over six hours since their capture.

Each time Ventosa tried to plead their case, a spear tip was pressed into his larynx. The captors were studying the plant sketch as if it were the secret of the universe. Ventosa and Preston were back to back against a tree and could not see each other.

Presently, an older Indian emerged from the trail. Judging by his face paint and attire, Preston surmised him to be their shaman. He took the plant sketch from one of the other men and studied it, turning it around in his hands. He spoke to the others in harsh tones. In response, they showed him the captured men's bags. In Ventosa's they found a .38 special revolver, fully loaded. They'd seen such an item before.

The shaman proceeded to conduct a lengthy interrogation of the two warriors, wherein they explained what exactly had transpired. Preston and Ventosa listened in, unable to glean any meaning from the rapid-fire diatribe.

"What do you think?" whispered Preston.

"Don't know," replied Ventosa. "My gun didn't help."

"What do they suspect?"

"This is their territory, we're the intruders. They've come to be suspicious of any or all visitors and I can't say I blame them."

"Boy, things sure have changed," whispered Preston. He could remember as recently as a few years ago traveling alone in this general region, befriending the natives as he went. The suspicious, potentially violent behavior of this tribe suggested to him that something dramatic had changed them. "What caused the new attitude?"

"Oil. Greed. Lack of respect," replied Ventosa.

"Is it really that widespread? I mean, this is so far into the interior."

"These lands haven't been fouled yet and they want to keep it that way. They've learned to defend themselves."

"How can we convince them we're not looking for oil deposits?"

"We're in deeper shit than that, I'm afraid."

"Why?"

"The sketch."

"What sketch?" Preston didn't get it.

"The plant. Their sacred tea."

"Oh shit." Preston got it then. Oil was one thing, ayahuasca was another. One simply didn't mess with the sacred tea of the Amazon. On the one hand, it was good news. It meant that perhaps the tribe's men recognized the sketch as a rendition of one of the plants used in their ayahuasca, which would confirm that Preston was getting warm. On the other hand, assuming there was no good reason for Ventosa and Preston to be hunting the sacred plants anyway, their lives were definitely in danger.

The shaman had left several hours ago, leaving the original two guards. Finally, he reemerged from the trail. He approached the captives, then silently walked around them. The silence was deafening. He then approached the guards and barked a few orders, handing each an arrow he had carried with him.

"What's with the arrows?" Preston asked.

"Poison, I'm guessing."

"For us?"

"One would assume."

"What kind of poison?" asked Preston, his botanical curiosity aroused.

"Hard to say. Each tribe has its own version, all different from the rest. Some lethal, some not."

Just then the shaman approached them. The guards had drawn the arrows taut on their bows, aiming at Preston and Ventosa. Without saying a word, the shaman sliced through the ropes at their feet, then their hands. He eyed them disdainfully, then with a strong, sharp gesture of his right arm, pointed for them to go.

Glancing quickly at the drawn arrows, the frightened men took off along the trail.

"Run goddammit! Don't look back!" shouted Ventosa. Just then he heard the unmistakable whistle of an arrow. He felt it fly past his arm, and heard it land in a tree. Preston wasn't so lucky.

The arrow pierced his leg right above the knee, knocking him to the ground. He grasped the arrow shaft, and with a loud scream, pulled hard. The shaft dislodged from the head, which stayed embedded in the flesh of his leg, courtesy of a barbed tip. He tried quickly to dig it out, causing only more pain. It was lodged.

Ventosa looked back quickly and saw what had transpired with Preston. He stopped and ran to help his friend.

"Come on. We'll look at it later." He helped him up and with Preston's arm over his shoulder, headed down the trail. Ventosa concluded that they weren't being followed, as slow as they hobbled they'd be easy prey. It meant the arrow was meant to do the job...

"How do you feel?"

"Fine, really, except for this arrow in my damn leg."

"I'm sure it hurts."

"If it's poison, I sure can't tell."

Ventosa slowed to a stop then helped Preston onto a felled tree. There he looked closely at the embedded arrowhead.

"Shit."

"What?"

"Delay arrow."

"What?"

"It's a timed release mechanism. Very clever."

"Please explain."

Ventosa was poking around to double check his theory. "See this?" He was sticking the tip of his pocket knife blade into the center of the arrowhead where the shaft had been. It was filled with a waxy substance.

"What about it?"

"Piloba wax. The poison is embedded inside the wax plug. Your body heat will melt the wax, releasing the poison."

"What's the point?"

"This way, the intruder can get away for a short while pointing the way to the enemy camp. It's a way to…"

"OH." Preston moaned, his head falling backward.

"Marty! Marty!" Ventosa slapped his friend's face. Preston was out, although still breathing. Ventosa looked around. He guessed they were one hundred yards from the river. It was his only

hope.

Chapter 56

Antidote

The fisherman lazily steered his boat down the river, deftly

maneuvering past fallen trees and rocks. He had speared two fish,

which would provide meals for a few days to supplement the

cassava. Suddenly, as his boat rounded an oxbow heading north, he noticed the two men struggling on the beach. One of them was seemingly unconscious, the other, upon seeing the boat, began waving his arms wildly.

"Help! Help!" shouted Ventosa.

The fisherman responded by picking up his bow and stretching an arrow into place.

"Please. No harm." Ventosa held up his arms as if to signify that he was unarmed. Actually, he was, since leaving his bag at the previous camp when they escaped. He pointed to Preston and shouted, "poison arrow."

The fisherman swung his boat wide against the current to get a closer look. Indeed, the white man had a protruding arrowhead in his leg. Fresh blood still poured from the wound, indicating its recent origin. Ventosa grabbed the bow of the boat as it hit shore.

"We haven't much time." Ventosa spoke in native tongue. He pointed off to the right where smoke from the village fires was billowing above the canopy. The point of the river where they stood was at the vortex of a fork in the river. The branch Ventosa pointed to led to Bitu's village, one half hour away. To the left, heading due west and several hours away, was the fisherman's village.

He was obviously fishing in hostile waters.

"No. Bitu. No go," he said, referring to the feared shaman.

"What? No, you don't understand."

"No go," the fisherman hurriedly tried to break away from the bank and head home. Sensing the loss of his last hope, Ventosa leaped forward, striking the surprised fisherman with a powerful backfist to the face. Stunned, the fisherman fell into the river. Ventosa followed, kicking him in the head. His lights went out.

Quickly, he dragged the fisherman's body onto shore and grabbed Preston.

"Help," the botanist moaned. "Help me."

"We're getting help. Hang in there." It was difficult dragging Preston's limp body onto the unstable boat. With much effort, Ventosa was able to get into the hull and he pushed off, heading for Bitu's village. He wondered what the fisherman had feared so much at the mention of Bitu's village.

The boat was much more difficult to maneuver than Ventosa could've imagined. Several times he nearly tipped the craft attempting to avoid debris and more than once he had the boat turned completely in the wrong direction. Ventosa's ineptitude was unnoticed by his passenger, who lay prostrate in the center of the boat. By now Preston was feverish and mumbling.

Ventosa spotted the village and struggled against the current to reach shore. Once there, he shouted for help.

Two teenage members of the tribe approached the boat cautiously. When they saw the downed Preston, they ran to help him ashore. Immediately, the younger boy ran off in search of more help. Within minutes several men, including Bitu, John and McCloud accompanied him.

They huddled around the victim. Ventosa spoke up.

"Poison arrow. Slow release, taking effect now." He said simply, not thinking that McCloud and John could understand his English. He was still confused about their presence to begin with.

"The plant. Got to find the plant," Preston mumbled.

"What's he saying?" asked McCloud.

"Something about a plant," said John.

Bitu examined the arrowhead carefully. "Piloba. Very deadly."

McCloud crowded next to him. "Piloba?"

"Type of wax, poison mixed in. Releases slowly in the system," Ventosa said, answering the question.

"Anything you can do?" asked McCloud.

"Swenson needs isolate. Help me find isolate," Preston mumbled.

"What isolate? Who needs it?"

"Swenson needs isolate."

"Swenson? Who's Swenson?" McCloud pressed.

"Wood. Wood needs it."

"Wood? What Wood?"

Preston turned his head and fell silent. Bitu hurried to his hut and emerged with a small container with a few ounces of a black liquid.

"Antidote," he announced. Holding Preston's mouth open, he poured it in slowly, rubbing Preston's throat to make him swallow. Preston responded by coughing.

"Swenson. Wood. What the devil is going on here?" asked McCloud. He turned to Ventosa.

"Who are you?"

"Ventosa. At your service," said the guide.

"And your friend?"

"Marty Preston. Scientist. We're looking for plants."

"What kind of plants?"

"Used in the tea."

"Yage?"

"Yes."

"Why?"

"We were hired."

"By who?"

"I don't know. Just the guide."

Just then Preston regained some degree of consciousness. He was in a hazy, dreamlike state caused by the lingering effects of the arrow toxin.

"What are you doing in this region, my good man?" asked McCloud.

"Finding plant. So close. So close."

"What the hell is he talking about?" he asked Ventosa.

"I believe he was sent by a pharmaceutical company to find a drug plant. Supposedly it has something to do with yage."

McCloud looked over to Bitu. No words were exchanged, but it was obvious that they were connecting on that thought.

"What pharmaceutical company is interested in yage?"

"I don't know. I'm just the guide. He said something the other day...Wood labs, I believe. Does that make any sense?"

McCloud gazed off into infinity. "Swenson! What the hell is he up to?" He patted Preston on the cheek. "Wake up! Wake up!"

Preston rolled his head, opening his eyes slightly. He was conscious, but very incoherent. "The plant. Isolate the plant away from the tea."

"What the devil . . . What plant?" he asked Ventosa again.

"Wait a second. Here, I almost forgot," he said, pulling the tattered plant sketch from his pocket. "I believe this is it."

McCloud took the sketch over to Bitu, who examined it closely. They engaged in a deep discussion, overheard by no one. It was obvious that Bitu recognized the plant from the sketch.

"You must not allow this plant to leave the forest," Bitu commanded Ventosa in a menacing voice.

Chapter 57

Goin' Down Slow

President Reagan stood before dozens of blinding lights, with flashes going off relentlessly. The Great Communicator was doing what he does best--pleasing the crowd. He had accepted the invitation to speak before the delegation of Red Cross Volunteers, converging in San Diego for their annual convention. It was apparent by his opening remarks, however, that he had either never heard of the Red Cross or he had completely forgotten where he was.

As the host announced the guest of honor, the Secret Service agents ushered the President and First Lady to the podium amid thunderous applause. After smiling and waving for several minutes, the President took his place at the microphone while the First Lady sat down close by, at the head table where she joined the high ranking national delegation of the Red Cross Volunteers. Gradually the applause died down and the President cleared his throat.

"Good afternoon ladies and gentlemen. It is very much an honor to address such a worthy organization as the Salvation Army."

Silence.

There was an uncomfortable moment of seat squirming among the audience members, most of whom waited anxiously for an indication that he tried to slip a joke into his opening statement. It was no joke.

Stunned, Nancy reached over and grabbed her husband's hand. He bent down putting his ear to her mouth. In the process, she attempted to correct him, but apparently he wasn't comprehending it.

"Nancy has just reminded me, and I agree wholeheartedly, that it is the greatest of honors to bestow upon several of your volunteers the revered Red Cross Medal . . .er . . .certainly a monumental achievement."

At this Nancy stood up and gently urged her husband back from the microphone stand. They stood talking for several minutes, the President looking somewhat confused. Finally, Nancy summoned one of the Secret Service men and the press secretary. After a brief conference, the President was led off the stage and the Press Secretary took the microphone.

"Excuse me, ladies and gentlemen. I regret to inform you that the President has quite suddenly taken mildly ill, and will have to delay his speech for a few minutes. We apologize for any inconvenience. In the interim, we will turn the mike back over to

John Palmer, the master of ceremonies for the convention. Thank you."

As he left, the audience erupted in a confused, hushed babble. The President would not, as it turned out, return to the stage that day.

"Can we have some water please?" The First Lady demanded. She was seated on a davenport with the confused Commander in Chief.

"The doctor is on his way." Agent Clarke walked over to check on them.

"I'm fine, really. I don't know that the fuss is all about," said the President.

"Honey, you forgot your speech entirely. You even forgot whom you were speaking to! There was nothing I could do to help you."

Reagan shook his head. "Really, I think everyone's over reacting."

"Let's just wait to see what the doctor says." She comforted him.

"I don't want to disappoint them. The AMVETS are such a wonderful organization."

"Gibbons here." He answered in one ring.

"We had another incident."

"Where? What?"

"The Red Cross convention in San Diego. This morning. He thought they were the Salvation Army."

"Oh shit!"

"We took him off stage before there was too much damage."

"It doesn't take much at this point."

"We need to intervene soon. What's going on with your research?"

"It's moving along. We need to accelerate the human testing."

"Do what you have to. But we need to do something, and not a minute to spare."

"Understood." Gibbons hung up. *What the devil is going on, he thought.* It was agreed that there would be no radio communications between him and McCloud. Now he was sorry that they were in blackout.

It was Saturday night. Supposedly, the McCloud Team would be returning the next day. But if something went wrong, the delay could be damaging. Reagan was scheduled to leave for Geneva in thirty days for his International Nuclear Freeze Summit. If something was going to be done it had to be done now.

"Carla?"

"Yes sir?"

"I need to schedule an immediate flight to Brazil. Classified. And get Perez on the line."

"Yes sir." Carla Smith had been his personal secretary for twelve years and was indispensable. Rinaldo Perez was Gibbons' most trusted field agent in the Amazon region. Lately he'd been out of fieldwork, but now his expertise in the rain forest was needed badly.

"Mr. Perez on the line, sir," came Carla's soft voice.

"Thank you." Gibbons hit the other line. "Rinaldo."

"Yes sir. How are you?"

"Fine, thank you. I need your help."

"I'm listening."

Gibbons proceeded to explain in detail the objectives of

McCloud's mission and the urgency.

"Sounds exciting," said Rinaldo.

"You available?"

"You tell me I need to go and I'm available for you. You know

that."

"Thank you. Can you be at the airport at nineteen hundred?"

"West terminal?"

"As always."

"Yes sir. Nineteen hundred it is."

Gibbons couldn't tell for sure, but it sounded like he made

Perez' day. He grabbed his prepared overnight bag and headed out.

"Leaving the country?" Carla asked.

"Brazil. Back tomorrow."

"Need a date?" For years she and Gibbons had acted out he roles of James Bond and his secretary, Moneypenny. It helped ease the tensions of the job.

"Not this time. I'm taking Perez."

"Oh well. Have fun. He's not as fun as I can be."

"Thanks." He smiled at her. Unfortunately, this mission was far too serious to think about fun. He just didn't know how serious.

Chapter 58

Plans Revealed

"I'm sorry sir. There's nothing we can do right now."

Gibbons was staring into the eyes of the airport official. Apparently, a DC9 on approach from Atlanta had to make an emergency landing due to inoperable landing gear. It was due in one hour, but the preparations had begun and all flights suspended until further notice. Not even the CIA could override the FAA.

"How long?" Gibbons knew there was no way around the delay.

"Could be a couple of hours. Depends on how ugly their landing turns out."

Gibbons looked at Perez. "Come on. I'll need an interpreter."

Perez followed the CIA commander out of the restricted concourse of the airport. They hustled to the parking lot where

Gibbons' van was parked. "We can try the phone, but I'll need your Portuguese tongue to break through the international screen."

"He doesn't have a two way?"

"Negative. They had to travel light. Besides, we didn't expect to have to make any communications. They took a standard military issue field phone for emergencies. But it usually doesn't get through without some interference. That's where you'll come in."

"What's that?" Craig asked. There was a beeping noise emanating from somewhere around McCloud's tent.

"I don't know. I'll go get McCloud." John departed.

"I still can't believe it," said Kelly, holding her content baby. Jason hadn't cried his usual colicky way since the tea therapy.

"You think he's really cured?" asked Craig.

"This is the longest he's gone without crying. It's weird."

"How about you?" he asked.

"I'm fine. It was quite an experience, but I don't know what to think yet."

Craig was shaking his head, standing in the doorway of the hut.

"What's wrong?" she asked him.

"Nothing. Nothing at all." He turned around to look her in the eyes. "Something happened to me too during that session."

"Like what?"

"I got a clear message. Like suddenly I knew that I was on the wrong path."

"Maybe you're overreacting."

"No. Definitely not. I was totally out of place. And you know something? I think I've known it all along."

"What are you saying, Craig?"

"I think I'm going to stay here. For a while, anyway." He paused. "Didn't that tea have any effect on you?"

She thought about it for a minute. "I don't know. I mean, I didn't know what to expect. They said I got a lower dose, anyway."

"Wow, wait a minute."

"What?"

"Why would you get a lower dose compared to me?"

"Could it be that I weigh half as much as you do?"

"Hey." He grabbed his inner tube belly. "Not exactly half. Anyway, my dose was way more than double yours. Like something was in the works…I'll be right back." With that he was gone, leaving a perplexed Kelly sitting with her baby in the steamy hut.

Craig approached McCloud's tent and could hear a conversation. It was McCloud, Bitu and John. There was also a crackling voice that sounded as if it were being transmitted from a great distance. He hid nearby in some brush to eavesdrop.

"Charlton. Do you read me?" The voice crackled.

"Ten four Colonel. Can you boost?"

"It is Gibbons?" Bitu asked.

"Yep. He wanted to pay us a visit, but ran into some travel complications."

"How did things go?" asked Gibbons.

"Beautifully. The child is cured and the mom is doing well."

"Who's in earshot?"

"Bitu and Masters. Mr. Hunt is with Kelly."

"How did he fare?"

"Very well," John interjected. "Our dose was high, but he came out all right."

Craig was stunned. He moved closer.

"Can we proceed with the plan?" Gibbons asked.

"Absolutely," replied Bitu. Suddenly he didn't sound all that much like a primitive Amazonian medicine man.

"Which plan?" asked the colonel.

"Operation Tea Babies. The adult results are too inconsistent for general use. We can go ahead with Reagan and a few selected others, but for the general use let's stick to colic."

"What are you talking about?" asked John.

"Masters?" asked Gibbons.

"Yes sir."

"This is classified, son, but we may need your help."

"Go ahead."

"Charlton, I think it would be easier for you to explain this mess."

"OK. Here goes." He looked at John. "You ready?"

John nodded.

McCloud swept his arm in a wide arc. "This was one small area of the rain forest. However, it's important for two reasons. Strategically, it marks a boundary for oil encroachment. Beyond here, great oil reserves await the oil drillers. The forest would be gone in a matter of years. If they can't get past, we have a chance."

"Makes sense."

"Secondly, some of the plant life in this region is truly unique. Especially the ingredient used in Bitu's tea."

"It's that different from other ayahuasca?"

Bitu simply nodded.

"Our friend here knew through his visions that something drastic would be necessary to overcome the political power of the oil companies in order to save his beloved forest lands."

"Like money?"

"Yes. But more money than anyone had to spend, at least except for another industrial interest besides oil."

"Like what?"

"Pharmaceuticals," McCloud continued. "The theory was that as soon as we developed a major drug from this region, the revenue would be able to overpower the oil interests. Drug development is big business, sometimes bigger than oil."

"So, you're looking to market the tea?" John asked incredulously.

"Sort of. There were two approaches we studied, both with huge market potential. The first was cortical enhancement, the second infant colic."

"Not very similar," John noted.

"No. And Bitu was more in favor of the infant colic approach. For that, the regular tea could be used in low doses. The cortical enhancement seemed promising for Alzheimer's, but so far there had been no success in isolating the constituent responsible for neuronal enhancement proliferation. The problem was that the tea was too strong from the hallucinogenic standpoint to make it acceptable. Bitu has since warned us that trying to separate the individual compounds was too dangerous.

"Is that what the other botanist was doing?"

"What botanist?" demanded Gibbons.

"We had a visitor. Swenson sent his own team down here."

"You're kidding! What happened?"

"He stumbled into camp with an arrow wound. He had a plant sketch of one of Bitu's secret ingredients. Apparently it was drawn by Temple's assistant during a tea vision and Swenson got a hold of it at Wood before firing Temple."

"Where's he now?"

"Recovering. I don't think he's much of a threat."

"Be careful with him. Swenson's a tough egg."

"Ten four."

McCloud continued. "At any rate, the colic theory needed to be tested, which we did yesterday. Temple feels confident that he can reproduce the results in the lab. As far as cortical enhancement, the CIA is still very interested. There was no doubt that ayahuasca stimulated neuronal network proliferation. The trick was to find the right dose. We tried that on you and Craig yesterday, and the results were favorable enough for us to try the ultimate test."

"Which is?"

"The Geneva Summit. We feel ayahuasca will stimulate Reagan just enough to get through the vital issues."

"Is this a joke?" John asked.

"Absolutely not. At first we thought we could study the mind enhancement aspects over a wide selection of adults, but it soon became obvious that its use would be limited. However, we had our backs to the wall and decided to go ahead with it anyway. Small doses. We had it narrowed down to two, which was decided between you and your friend."

"Wow!"

"I know it sounds hard to believe."

"Where to from here?"

"We take the colic test back to the states, where Dr. Temple will spearhead a drug development project financed by the NSC. We hope to market that within five years."

"Rather soon for a new drug, isn't it?"

"We have connections with the FDA," smiled McCloud.

"And the President?"

"Colonel Gibbons will fulfill project R.O.N. in two days by administering a small dose of ayahuasca to President Reagan before the summit. By sustaining the President's mental capacity we hope to guide him through the end of his term, which will stabilize the global economy making our endeavor less risky."

"You have this all planned out," John said, amazed.

"Oh, yes. It's been in the works for many years."

"We'll look for you tomorrow then?" Gibbons cut in.

"As scheduled. We'll board in the morning."

"Count me out," said Craig as he entered the hut.

Chapter 59

Encounter

"Not home?" Bob Timmons was knocking on Craig's door and had to turn around to see whom it was that asked. It was Kyle Ferguson.

"Excuse me?" Bob asked.

"He's not home. Hasn't been for days," Kyle said.

"Who are you?"

"Kyle Ferguson. Kelly's husband."

Bob was dumbfounded on the inside but kept a cool exterior. He sensed hostility, but didn't quite know why. Ferguson was certainly not an intimidating man, but his presence there was a surprise and the cause of his visit was anything but cordial.

"Nice to meet you. Bob Timmons." Bob stepped off the front porch to shake Kyle's hand. Kyle refused the gesture. "Have you been trying to get a hold of Craig also?"

"In a manner of speaking," Kyle said gruffly. His eyes were dulled and glassy from lack of sleep, his face unshaven. He'd taken off work since the disappearance of his family and had taken on the appearance of a disheveled drunkard.

Bob's mind was racing. All the possibilities that entered his mind were less than savory. But if there was something going on between Craig and Kelly, Bob was completely unaware of it. He had simply stopped by Craig's to say hello. And if Craig was gone, possibly for days, and this guy was looking for his wife, also gone . . .

Suddenly he wished he hadn't come to visit Craig.

"Where did your friend take my wife?" Kyle asked menacingly.

"I don't know what you are talking about."

"Oh no?"

"Look, I just stopped by to say hello to a friend. Is that a crime?"

"No. But kidnapping is."

"Look. If it's all the same to you, I'll just go back to where I came from and we'll forget all about this little meeting." Bob started walking past Kyle toward his car. The doctor put a strong grip on Bob's arm.

"No. Wait. Please." Kyle's tone suddenly changed. Bob looked at Kyle's grip and he let go.

"Can we talk?"

"Sure." Bob was totally perplexed.

"I didn't mean to be an ass," Kyle began. "My wife and child have been missing for two days now, and I think your friend might in some way be involved. Quite frankly, my wife may have gone on her own volition."

"What can you tell me?" Bob asked.

Kyle then proceeded to tell the whole story as he knew it. When he finished there was silence.

"Make any sense to you?"

Bob thought for a moment. It was obvious from Kyle's story that he already knew quite a lot. Bob felt that he couldn't lie to the man. Besides, he knew Craig and John were not trying to perform any diabolical stunt with Kelly.

"Yes," he stated. "I knew of a plan to go to Brazil for a therapy session with a medicine man there. Supposedly they have a drug which cures colic."

"Ayahuasca," Kyle said stoically.

"You know about it?"

"Some. I was just beginning to research it."

"So you think Kelly went with them to Brazil?" Bob asked.

"I have a sinking suspicion. There's no other possibility that I care to think about."

"You're a doctor, right?"

"Yes." Kyle replied.

"What's your take on the ayahuasca therapy?"

"I don't know. I know that it's used extensively in that region of the world, but it sounds more like witchcraft than medicine."

"Let's suppose for a minute that Kelly did take your baby to Brazil to try this ayahuasca, and say that it cured his colic. Where would you stand?"

"A cure is a cure. No matter how unorthodox. I only wish I'd had more say in how it was accomplished."

"The repercussions would be rather significant. Seems like there's a lot of colicky babies around."

"I agree. If someone discovered a cure for it they'd be instant heroes. Actually, the theory behind ayahuasca's mechanism of action makes a lot of sense."

"Would it catch on in this country if it worked?"

"Oh I think so. There's a growing support for herbal medicine right now. It would be very interesting to say the least. The thing that gets me is how these supposed primitives were able to solve a medical mystery that our modern techno-society didn't have a clue."

"Yeah, I agree. With thousands of plants it seems hard to believe that trial and error was their method," Bob mused.

"Impossible I would say."

"Legend says that the vine which produces the drug communicates these things to those who ingest it. Who can argue with that?" said Bob.

"Pretty heavy, but you're right. How else can we explain it?" Kyle and Bob were now getting along like old friends.

"Your friends," Kyle began, "They're good dudes?"

"Craig and John? Yeah, they're good guys. If your wife and kid are with them, then they're in good shape."

"Supposing they did go down, how long do you think it would be for?"

"Not long. Two or three days tops. Craig is walking on eggshells getting his law practice started. I don't think he'd do anything to jeopardize that."

"Like kidnapping a mother and child?" Kyle laughed. "Just kidding. Anyway, I'm too tired to look anymore. If the police haven't found any sign of foul play then I guess I'll accept the fact that she's probably in Brazil."

"If I hear from them I'll call you. Try to relax, get some rest. This will all shake out real soon," Bob reassured him.

"You're probably right. And if my son comes back without colic, I'll be ready to kiss the ground that shaman walks on."

Chapter 60

Sacred Grove

The Mubati are generally not an aggressive people. As acculturation continues, the occasional visit by white men becomes less and less unusual. In many cases, owing to the wonderful trade items introduced to them, the villagers welcome the strangers with open arms. So it is not surprising that Preston and Ventosa were left to their own devices while Preston recovered from the arrow poison.

By late Saturday night, Preston was feeling well enough to ease himself off his straw mat and stretch his aching muscles. In the inky blackness of the jungle he crept around the hut looking for the spot where Ventosa slept. Just as he found the empty straw mat, Ventosa entered the tent.

"Marty?" he asked seconds before bumping into his companion.

"Where have you been?" asked Preston.

"Sit down. I've learned some interesting information." He practically shoved Preston down.

"What's going on?"

"I was eavesdropping on the Americans here."

"Who?"

"Don't you remember?" Ventosa asked, slightly concerned.

"Not really. The whole thing seems like a dream, or a nightmare."

"The shaman here in this village saved your life. I brought you here after you were struck by the arrow."

"This is a different village?"

"Of course." Ventosa looked at his friend in the light of a candle they'd lit. The villages probably looked similar to an outsider, but he was amazed by Preston's apparent amnesia. "Are you sure you're feeling OK?"

"I'm fine. Now, let's get out of here."

"What do you mean? Right now?"

"Right now. We've got work to do."

Ventosa's first thought was to try and talk Preston out of it. But the more he thought about it, the more sense it made to get moving. There was no guarantee of their safety in this village. Preston was already packed and ready to go.

"All right. You're the boss." Ventosa gathered his few belongings and they left after blowing out their candle.

Preston followed as Ventosa carefully made his way to the river. The well-worn path was fairly well outlined but it was still very dark. On more than one occasion Preston tripped over a rock or a tree branch. Finally they make it to the water's edge.

Moored at the beach were four dug out canoes. A thin crescent moon was just visible overhead, and as Preston's eyes grew accustomed to the darkness it provided enough light to see fairly well. Ventosa was already untying one of the canoes and loading their packs.

"Come on. You can look at the moon from the canoe," he said impatiently.

"Where the hell are we going in the middle of the night, anyway?" Preston joked.

"Down river," came Ventosa's uninformative response. " This was your idea, remember?"

They traveled in silence for over an hour. Ventosa requested that they not talk so as not to attract attention. The dawn glow was already beginning to bathe the eastern horizon. Preston could make out some of the details of the riverbank.

"What's that, up ahead?" he whispered.

Up to the left was a definite clearing, although there was no sign of a village. It looked like a little beach in the middle of nowhere.

"Don't know. Want to investigate?" Ventosa asked.

"Sure."

The small craft made it to the beach and Ventosa hopped out to secure it to the nearest tree. The morning birds were already singing as the other jungle animals began to awaken, or in the case of nocturnal hunters, head back home. The beach narrowed into a well-trodden path, but still no village was evident.

"Could be hunting path," said Ventosa. He bent down to examine the ground. "Fresh tracks . . .two days at most."

They continued on. About three hundred yards into the forest they came across a clearing, which upon closer inspection took on the appearance of an unusual garden. Groups of plants appeared to have been cultivated, neatly separated from each other and from the surrounding foliage.

"Bingo," said Preston. He had immediately recognized the majestic Banisteriopsis lianas powerfully ascending to the canopy. Next to them in a separate patch was a group of plants, which revealed themselves as psychotria viridis. Next to them, the hallucinogenic Banisteriopsis Rusbyana. Preston knew each grouping of plants, neatly cultivated, as one of several ingredients used in the preparation of ayahuasca. He was in a state of animated euphoria as he examined each.

"You think the plant is here?" Ventosa asked. He looked around nervously. Preston either didn't hear him or was too busy to reply. He had his sketch out and was comparing it to several species that he didn't immediately recognize.

"Ventosa! Over here!" he shouted. Ventosa ran over. Preston was holding the sketch up to a small bushy plant with waxy green leaves. Even to Ventosa's untrained eye, the plant matched the sketch perfectly.

"Oh senor, we've struck gold."

All Preston could do was smile. Carefully, he extracted a leaf and bit into it. The instantly bitter taste signaled the presence of alkaloids, the first hint that the plant contained medically active constituents. With the skill of years of experience, Preston began sampling the plant, collecting specimens into his pack. His portable plant press would preserve them at least as long as the trip home.

"OK, my friend. We're out of here."

"What about the shaman's warning?" Ventosa joked about overhearing Bitu's foreboding statement about removing that plant from the jungle.

"I'll take my chances," Preston stated, and hurried back to the path. After walking several yards, he looked back to ask Ventosa a question, but his guide was not following.

"Jose? Ventosa?" Preston walked slowly back to the garden. Before he was able to utter another word, the flesh on the back of his neck and shoulders was torn open. The blow knocked him down, and before the deathblow Preston could feel the warmth of his own

blood spilling down his back.

Chapter 61

Mission Accomplished

Kelly awoke Sunday morning a new woman. At first she believed that her feelings of energized euphoria were the result of Jason having slept through the whole night allowing her to do the same, giving her the best night's sleep she'd had in recent memory. But she realized there was more to it than that simple explanation. She felt cleansed and buoyant, as though on a drug high without the side effects. In short, she felt better and more alive than she'd ever felt in her life.

Craig and John had already packed their gear and set it neatly by the entrance to their hut. There was quietude unlike anything she had ever experienced. The hut was situated beneath the towering canopy and thereby afforded protection from the blazing sun. The jungle had proven to be a far different place than she had imagined it to be. The insects and wild animals had hardly factored into their journey, and although the facilities were primitive by her standards she never felt uncomfortable. On the contrary, she almost felt as though she could stay there forever.

Craig, too, felt that way. Unlike Kelly, though, Craig's sentiments were so powerful along those lines that he had made a daring decision to return to these woods. His decision was based, in part, on an invitation. Bitu, McCloud and Temple had begun formulating the foundation for their research project involving ayahuasca's development and marketing. It was decided that they needed some manpower in the Amazon to coordinate their efforts. John had volunteered, of course, and in the process realized that Craig would be an obvious choice as well. When approached with the offer, Craig needed only a few moments to decide. Like Kelly, he had noticed a transformation in himself, as if for the first time in his life he felt centered and happy, and he knew his return to the grindstone of law practice would erase those feelings.

Kelly picked up Jason as he awoke, cooing instead of crying. She was anxious to get home and share the amazing experience with Kyle. She believed his open mindedness would overpower any feelings of anger. Besides, his scientific curiosity would be on overtime as he examined his son.

Stepping out into the blazing sun, covering Jason with a light receiving blanket, she headed down the path towards the center of the village. All was quiet. Within minutes she was greeted by her travel companions.

"Good morning." McCloud was the first to greet her.

"Good morning."

Craig walked up and lifted the blanket, which partially covered Jason's face. The infant smiled.

"It's a miracle," Kelly said.

"Just the tip of the iceberg," McCloud said without elaborating. Their gear was already loaded onto the boats. All that remained to do was say goodbye. Kelly felt strangely resistant to the idea of leaving this wonderful and magical place. It was indeed the scene of a three-day adventure that changed her life completely.

As the group made its rounds of good byes and good lucks, Kelly noticed Bitu approaching her and Jason. As he glided toward her, Kelly decided that he was the most extraordinary man she'd ever met. His warm yet piercing eyes, calm face and graceful movements projected an image of a man so at ease with himself and his surroundings that she felt inadequate and insecure, as if she were so far away from that harmony. However, she reveled in the knowledge that through Bitu's living example, the same balance could be achieved in her own life as well.

She instinctively bowed her head as he approached then looked up into his eyes.

"You OK?" he asked.

"Yes. Wonderful."

He looked at Jason's contented face. "And you, my son, feel OK?" He gently stroked Jason's abdomen. Jason's smile broadened. "You are the first."

Kelly wondered if there was a deeper message there. "Thank you," she said to the shaman.

"Thank you." He held her hand gently. "Thank you from all of us." He gestured to the rest of the tribe who had gathered to say good bye.

She was speechless, and no matter. Nothing more needed to be said.

"We leave now," barked the boatman. They were escorted to the boats, abruptly closing the book on their experience. As Kelly situated herself in the boat, she gazed at the shore. Looking on, seemingly in his own world yet projecting a major presence in his surroundings, was Bitu. He didn't move or speak, but Kelly received a message from him. Thanks again, and good luck.

Roger Temple had little time to reflect on his incredible journey to the Amazon. Within hours of their return, he found himself in a makeshift laboratory in Gibbons' office. Gibbons and McCloud were sipping coffee as they observed the scientist at work.

Although they had two weeks before the summit, the CIA wanted to test the ayahuasca formulation on the President several times. They had postulated several possibilities for accomplishing this. After reviewing the President's preferences in food and drink, the first test involved a specially flavored tea. However, the ayahuasca was so strong tasting that they couldn't mask its presence. Ice cream and sherbet worked fairly well, but the President didn't regularly consume either. Then Temple had a brainstorm. The President did have a favorite snack – jelly beans. A confused but agreeable confection maker was hired to teach Temple the fine art of making homemade jelly beans, and within hours he was expertly showing off to his CIA bosses.

"Looks good. How does it taste?" asked Gibbons, holding up a jellybean to the light. It reflected a most unusual shade of brown.

"Try it. It's a funky chocolate," Temple said.

Gibbons popped it in his mouth. Aside from a mild aftertaste, there was no indication that he had just ingested a tropical hallucinogen. "Good. Can I have another?"

McCloud and Temple looked at each other, shrugged their shoulders and dug in. The test worked. All that remained was to supply the President with a generous supply of high octane, Government Issue jelly beans.

The President reached for his ever-present candy dish. Pulling out a handful of his favorite confection, he filled his mouth with the jelly delights.

"Mmm." He pressed the intercom. "Remind me to take an extra supply of my jelly beans to Geneva."

Chapter 62

Anxious Return

The taxi pulled up in front of the Ferguson house. It was Sunday evening and the house looked cold and empty. Kelly had decided that it would be advisable to take a cab home from the airport rather than risk a confrontation between McCloud and Kyle. As it turned out, Kyle appeared not to be home anyway.

Kelly paid the driver, picked up her bags and then retrieved Jason. It made her nervous to drive without his car seat but took the chance anyway. Looking at her house, she was struck by the mundane quality it projected in comparison to the pristine wilderness she had just left. It had only been three days, but felt like much more of an extended absence. Nonetheless, it was good to be home.

Even Jason's eyes lit up as if to signify his pleasure in returning to familiar surroundings.

Entering the home, Kelly was shocked by the disarray. Kyle's normally neat habits had been completely tossed aside, the house looking more like a college fraternity house with beer cans and pizza boxes scattered about. Kelly immediately felt remorse.

After a quick shower and bath for Jason, she began to settle back into her routine. As if by magic, her curiosity about Kyle's whereabouts caused him to materialize in the doorway to their bedroom. She almost didn't recognize him.

Kyle's beard was coming in. He looked like he hadn't slept in days, which was partially true. His T-shirt was torn and stained, and he wore sweat pants not meant to be worn in public. Husband and wife simply stared at each other. After what seemed like an eternity, Kyle walked up and gave Kelly a bear hug. Tears welled up in her eyes as he pulled her even closer.

"Thank god you're OK," he said.

"I'm so sorry," she sobbed. "I didn't expect things to go this way."

Stepping back, he held his hands on her shoulders. "What happened?"

Kelly proceeded to tell Kyle about their journey, the magical forest and the characters in an almost surrealistic tale. Kyle listened mesmerized.

"They think he's cured?" he asked.

"I think so. He hasn't had a colicky cry for two days."

"Has he seemed OK otherwise? I mean, any side affects?"

"I haven't detected any. He's been an angel." As if he heard that remark, Jason opened his eyes. He'd been asleep on their bed. Kyle immediately sat down next to him.

"Hey buddy. Did you miss me?"

Jason recognized his daddy and smiled. Kyle reached out to hold him.

"I'm sure he missed you," Kelly said.

"Let me get a look at you. You feel better?" Kyle examined Jason in a manner exclusive to physicians. His son not only looked OK; he looked better than ever.

"So tell me about the tea," Kyle said to Kelly.

"It was gross. Tasting I mean."

"What did it feel like?"

"It was definitely weird. The whole scene. We sat in a small clearing in the forest, and the shaman performed all kinds of crazy rituals."

"Crazy to you, maybe. Did you experience any visions?"

"I think so. But they told me my dose was real low, so it may have just been the setting."

"This McCloud character, was he on the level?"

"He's a neat guy. Real gentleman. They all were. I think McCloud's a very sincere, wealthy man who wants to do something really rewarding with his money." She then looked her husband over. "Are you OK?"

"I'm OK," he said. "It's been a rough couple of days. The police have been looking for you, the airport security . . ."

"The police?" she interrupted.

"Of course. I didn't know if you were safe for not."

"I guess. I didn't even think about that."

"The airport security wasn't any help either."

"Not surprising. I'm sure the CIA took care of that."

"The CIA?" Kyle was surprised. Up to now, she hadn't mentioned the security agency.

"Yeah, I guess they worked with McCloud."

"I wonder what the CIA has to do with all this?"

Just then the phone rang. Kelly answered. "Hello?"

"Uh. Is this the Ferguson residence?"

"Yes it is. This is Kelly."

"Kelly Ferguson?"

"Yes. Who is this?"

"Detective Tyra, Logan Police. We're, um, looking for you."

"I'm right here."

"Is your husband there?"

"Just a sec." She handed Kyle the phone.

"This is Ferguson," he said, sounding very much like a movie actor.

"Ferguson, this is Tyra. What's going on?"

"As you can tell, Kelly's made it home safely."

"I think you have some explaining to do."

"I know. Can I swing by the station tomorrow?"

"Please." Tyra hung up.

"I don't think he's happy with us." Kyle laughed.

"Why? I mean, you did his job for him," she laughed. "By the way, I like the beard."

"Thanks. I'm thinking about keeping it."

"Mind taking shower?"

"No. I guess I'm due."

"I'll go fix something for dinner."

She was surprised but happy that Kyle's anger all but vanished upon hearing her tale. Indeed, his medical curiosity outstripped his negative emotions. As he undressed for his shower, the phone rang again.

"Hello?"

"Kyle Ferguson, please."

"This is he."

"Dr. Ferguson, this is Charlton McCloud. Are you familiar with my name?"

"I just heard all about you."

"Not everything, I trust. Anyway, I hope we didn't disrupt your life too much."

"Time will tell. What can I do for you?"

"I'd like to make you an offer you can't refuse."

Chapter 63

Pieces of the Puzzle

"You guys piss me off." Bob Timmons was exaggerating his anger after hearing Craig and John tell their tale. "You didn't call me."

"You wouldn't have come anyway," argued John.

"I know. But that's besides the point."

"You can go next time."

"Promise?"

"Promise. Now, get me another beer."

The gathering at Craig's was exuberant. Kelly and Jason had stopped by along with Kyle, and Bob arrived shortly thereafter. It appeared that any hard feelings harbored by Kyle over the incident had dissipated.

Craig had excused himself to answer the phone then announced to the gathering that McCloud and Temple were on their way. Kyle smiled to himself, knowing all along that they were coming over.

"So you going to tell me what's going on?" Bob pleaded.

"In time, in time," John teased.

"Oh, give me a break."

"Anyone want anything to drink?" Craig asked.

As he took their respective requests and headed for the kitchen, Kelly handed Jason to Kyle and headed off to help. Bob looked at the baby, then to Kyle.

"I take it you've got the answers to all your questions?" he asked, referring to their brief encounter.

"Not all of them, but they will be forthcoming."

"Yeah, who are McCloud and Temple, anyway?"

Before Kyle could plead ignorance, there was a knock at the door. Bob went to answer it and was greeted by two casually dressed men, one with a briefcase.

"You must be McCloud and Temple."

"The same. May we come in?"

Bob stepped back to allow them in. McCloud put out his hand.
"Carlton McCloud. Pleasure."

"Bob Timmons. The pleasure's mine."

"This is Dr. Roger Temple."

Temple shook Bob's hand. Immediately, both men gravitated
toward Jason. The happy infant smiled at them, and they turned
their attention to Kyle, who began to stand.

"Please sit. It's a pleasure to meet you, Dr. Ferguson."

"Nice to meet you finally. I guess I owe a debt of gratitude," he
said, nodding to Jason.

"The debt is ours. But I prefer to think of ourselves as partners."

"Indeed. I've thought about your offer and I accept."

Craig and Kelly had just returned and caught the last sentence.
Craig looked quizzically at John, who shrugged.

As they all settled in, Bob became childishly impatient.

"Are you going to fill me in or what?"

"Yes. Actually, we have a lot of material to cover," McCloud stated. "In fact, there's a lot that we still don't completely understand."

"They've been spying on us," said John.

"Yes we have. And I apologize for the sneakiness."

"Are you the CIA?" Bob asked.

"No, although we worked closely with them. Our organization is called the NSC and we're a private corporation. National Security Coalition."

"Why us?"

"Let me start from the beginning. Back in 1976, President Rios of Brazil, who was a strong U.S. ally, was assassinated. There was a well-documented report that the assassination was forewarned to the Presidential Consulate by a Catholic Missionary two days before the tragedy. Naturally, it was taken as a claim to a conspiracy, despite the missionary's insistence that he was warned by a shaman who had seen the crime through an ayahuasca induced vision. After an exhaustive investigation, the CIA concluded that the missionary's story was sincere, that he was the messenger and had no involvement in the assassination. Thus began in earnest a study of ayahuasca's possible clairvoyance inducing capabilities."

"By the CIA?" asked Craig.

"Yes. Actually, it was Dr. Temple here, hired by the CIA, that spear headed the research. The results were interesting, but in time the changing political climates of both Brazil and the US eroded any serious support to the research and it was shelved."

"I stayed on as a consultant to the CIA and about ten years later a research grant was proposed to study the possibility of developing mind enhancement drugs. Although my lab crew was unaware, the project was specifically aimed at boosting President Reagan's mental sharpness," Temple said. "At first, the project was discouraging, as there were few known drugs that can enhance brain function with no noticeable side effects. That's when I remembered the ayahuasca, and the possibility struck me that I might be able to isolate a substance from the tea that could increase cortical function without the intoxication. The preliminary tests showed the most promising tea to be that of the sample that we got from you." He pointed to John.

"Me?" he asked, astonished.

"That's right. Getting back to the clairvoyance issue, we were able to identify the shaman who made the stunning assassination prophecy. It was Bitu."

There was silence in Craig's family room as everyone exchanged glances.

"So he gave you the tea?"

"Indirectly. We didn't want to risk direct involvement, so we watched him closely and realized that he was supplying you with the tea. We eventually followed you here and stole a tiny sample for analysis. I believe the sample was sitting on that table." McCloud pointed to Craig's kitchen table.

"Incredible," Craig mumbled.

"Once we were convinced that Bitu's blend was the most active, we befriended him ourselves to get more." McCloud stood and paced before gaping mouths. "It seems that Bitu had a private agenda himself, based on visions triggered by John's association with Craig, and therefore to Kelly and Jason."

"What kind of agenda?" asked Kyle.

"Bitu knew that his forest was in trouble from oil drilling. He needed to facilitate the development of a drug that when marketed would provide capital to fight off the oil drillers."

"Cure for colic?"

"That's right. Bitu already knew it worked for his people, he just needed to convince the American researchers."

"What about mind enhancement?" Kyle asked.

"There was a tragedy," Temple said with difficulty. "My research assistant and I tried the tea. He had an unusual reaction that proved fatal and the research was called off. At least by Wood Pharmaceuticals, our major sponsor."

"What type of reaction: Hypersensitivity?"

"No, it was a cerebral hemorrhage. We had discounted the MAO inhibitive side effects completely, and didn't realize that my partner had eaten a tyramine rich meal that day." Temple had to stop for a moment. "He didn't die in vain, however. His death gave me the clue I needed. The ayahuasca contained MAO inhibitors for an as yet undiscovered receptor, MAO C, which may be the clue to its mind enhancement properties. I don't know anything more because the research was canceled, or so I thought."

"What do you mean?"

"Wood Pharmaceuticals apparently saw the potential, because they sent their own man to search out the tea."

"The one who stumbled into our camp?"

"Exactly."

"So Bitu was working with you all along?"

"We needed him and vice versa. I wouldn't say we were close. However, we've already set up a preliminary laboratory to start testing. We doubt there'll be any interference." McCloud paused, and looked at Kyle. "That's where you come in, if you choose to accept. We need a medical doctor to monitor our progress."

"So is Wood Pharmaceutical or any one else actively researching this strange mind effect?"

McCloud smiled at Temple. "We're not at liberty to say, but you'll know soon enough."

Chapter 64

At the Summit

Perhaps there was no more appropriate setting for the 1986

International Nuclear Freeze Summit than Reykjavik, Iceland. The

stark, gray weather and the stone buildings mimicked the moods of the delegations headed by President Reagan and his Russian counterpart Mikhail Gorbachev. It seemed that there would be no agreements, the two men worlds apart literally and figuratively. The lethargic and oft confused American leader seemed to annoy the charismatic and energetic Soviet reformer. Indeed, when the summit ended there was little progress made toward the historic treaty.

One year later, President Reagan relaxed in the Oval office. He reached instinctively for his jellybeans, his famous weakness. These were different, with a slightly woody taste that grew on him. He made a mental note to find out where these new beans came from.

Then something strange happened. The summit briefing, sixty pages of international legal jargon, suddenly took on a life of their own. The documents, which normally fatigued his eyes and brain, became fascinating. Each sentence was intriguing, each paragraph an earth shattering revelation. The President couldn't turn the pages quickly enough as he scooped handfuls of jellybeans into his mouth. The strange jellybeans reflected light differently. And they directed light into his world differently.

"This treaty proposal is marvelous," he thought aloud. Why had

he been so apathetic before?

He stood with an unusual grace and gravitated toward the

window overlooking the gardens and grounds of the White House.

The sweet smell of spring caressed his aging nostrils, blending

nicely with the aftertaste of jellybeans. After feeling lousy for so

long it was strange to feel good. Great. Young. He glanced at the

portraits on the wall, his predecessors. He'd often wondered how

they had dealt so energetically with the conflicts they faced. Wars.

Depressions. Scandals. He'd always felt insecure by comparison.

Until now. He turned to his desk, hurried to his chair needing only

its edge to sit on. Once again he immersed himself in documents.

He wanted the summit to begin now. "Now dammit," his fist

slamming the mahogany.

"Yes sir?"

His secretary heard. He'd left the intercom on by accident.

"Nothing. Er, sorry." Then in a flash of insight, "Please bring

the minutes from the last summit in Reykjavik."

"The synopsis sir?"

"No. The whole thing. Every detail."

"Sir?"

"I need to review every last detail. Please."

"Yes sir."

He couldn't wait to see the documents. The technical descriptions of the missiles in engineer's terminology. The geographic regions involved, their mountains and rivers. The cultures affected, their beliefs, hopes and dreams. He should have known all of this, but he didn't. He didn't know why, or how he'd come so far without such knowledge. It was time to catch up.

The documents were wheeled in. Nancy looked at her husband with confusion. He canceled his luncheon. He had some reading to do. Gorbachev would swing into town in seventy-two hours.

The Soviet Premier eyed his counterpart quizzically, his raised brow contorting the unique pigmentation on his forehead. Reagan was a ball of fire, asking questions based on extensive research. At times Gorbachev was sent scrambling, at a loss for details that to Reagan seemed common knowledge. He was confused but had no time to analyze. He'd come to Washington with a sound game plan, the upper hand in the delicate negotiations. But now his strategy was in shambles, plundered by an American leader whose mind was working leaps ahead of his own. He was out gunned, reeling from his own incompetence. He cursed at his advisors who groped ineptly for the answers to questions he did not- could not- have anticipated.

Through damage control, the Soviets were able to negotiate certain terms of the treaty that barely leveled the playing field. But they were exhausted and confused. Beaten by a master strategist who dominated the Summit as few Presidents ever have. And with the stroke of a pen, it was over.

Reagan looked up and out over the crowd. There were flashes of light. Applause. And he shook the hand of the curious looking man who had become his ally. At least on paper. Was it the end of the Cold War? If so, the spoils of victory would go to the newly revived American Commander in Chief.

One year later. 1988. Moscow. The International Nuclear Freeze Treaty was about

to be finalized. Once again, the Russian Premier found himself seated across the table from the supposedly aged American President. Gorbachev was startled. Reagan looked even younger, more vibrant. And although the Russian leader had boned up on the details of the treaty completion, he was still licking his wounds from the previous summit.

The stage was set. The preparations were made, and one hour remained until the opening of the meeting. Gorbachev stood and walked around the table to the surprise of the delegates. He approached the President and smiled. There was simple dialogue, courtesy of the official interpreters. There was laughter, even a pat on the back. Finally a gesture. The President motioned to a jar of jellybeans in front of him. Gorbachev smiled and declined. The President insisted. Finally, Gorbachev consented, reaching in to the jar and grabbing a few of the magical candies. He liked them.

"Take as many as you like. I've got plenty."

The Soviet leader agreed, grabbing a few more handfuls and returning to his seat. There, he glanced warmly at the President, and began to pop the jellybeans into his mouth.

+